LIZ HURLEY
UNCOVERED

LIZ HURLEY
UNCOVERED

Alison Bowyer

André Deutsch

First published in 2003 by
André Deutsch
An imprint of the
Carlton Publishing Group
20 Mortimer Street
London W1T 3JW

A catalogue record for this book is available from the British Library

ISBN 0 233 05116 3

The publishers would like to thank the following sources for their
kind permission to reproduce the pictures in this book:

Tim Rooke/Rex Features: p5 (top); Corbis: p6 (top); Robert
Knight/Corbis Sygma: p6 (bottom); Chris Weeks/BEI/Rex Features:
p7 (top); Rex USA Ltd/Rex Features: p7 (bottom); Andrew
Murray/Rex Features: p8 (top); www.splashnews.com: p8 (bottom)

Typeset by E-Type, Liverpool
Printed and bound in Great Britain by Mackays

Contents

Acknowledgements

The author would like to thank, among others: Antony Allcock, William Annesley, Tony Broccoli, Anita Brown, Matt Calais, Judith Chilcote, Birgit Cunningham, Chris Fleming, Marc Freden, Debra Holder, Henrietta Knight, Sean Macaulay, Paul Scott, Aileen Scriven, and the team at André Deutsch and Carlton Books.

1 The Godfather(s)

By anyone's standards, the christening of baby Damian Charles Hurley was never going to be a conventional affair. To start with, there was the child's radiant mother: her body polished and buffed to perfection and her already regained figure encased in a clinging white dress. Then there were the guests. Titled heirs to English castles mixed with the aristocracy of the pop world, while the Hollywood contingent was represented by a member of America's very own royalty – the billionaires' club. And instead of the usual pair of godparents, no less than six godfathers had been selected to keep a benevolent eye on the baby Damian. It may perhaps have behoved one of the godfathers to whisper in the infant's ear that when your mother is Elizabeth Hurley, you had better get used to being the focus of a great deal of attention.

It was ever thus. Even before his birth on April 4, 2002, young Damian had already been the subject of more column inches than a young royal. His warring parents, whose love affair had turned into one of the ugliest public slanging matches of modern times, had ensured that the months leading up to his birth had been unsettled, to say the least. And while there were men aplenty at the christening ceremony three months later in London, there was one male who was notably absent – the baby's father. Instead of being at his son's side on this most memorable of days, Stephen Bing was six thousand miles away at his home in Bel Air, California.

The christening was held at the Church of the Immaculate Conception in London's Mayfair, an ironic choice of venue given that Damian's conception could hardly have caused more consternation if it had indeed been a virgin birth. And despite the happy smiles of the christening contingent as they celebrated the baptism, young Damian's life could not have got off to a less happy start.

The circumstances surrounding the birth and paternity of Damian Hurley had been played out in the full glare of the international media spotlight. Almost from the very moment he was conceived – at Sir Elton John's sumptuous villa in the South of France – his parents had been at daggers drawn. And although little has actually been said on the subject by Elizabeth herself, and almost nothing at all by her former paramour, both sides ensured that their viewpoint was put in the public arena.

For her part, Liz maintained that she had fallen pregnant by accident when antibiotics she was taking interfered with the contraceptive pill. Rubbish, claimed Steve Bing's camp, she tricked him into fatherhood; he had been reproductively taken advantage of. It didn't help Elizabeth's case that the man she had become pregnant by just happened to be heir to a $400 million real estate fortune. No matter which way you looked at it, argued her critics, it did look suspiciously like the actions of a gold-digger.

Worse was to come. Steve Bing publicly questioned

Elizabeth's moral values by suggesting that he might not even be the father of the child she was carrying, and that they had not been in an exclusive relationship. Outraged by what they saw as a smear on her good name, Elizabeth's friends immediately hit back, accusing him of ungentlemanly behaviour and labelling him 'Bing Laden'.

The bitter war of words, including the claim that Bing had asked Elizabeth to have an abortion and accusations from his camp that she had taken part in a three-in-a-bed sex session, was all awarded the maximum publicity on television and in the Press. Elizabeth insisted throughout that there was no doubt in her mind that Steve Bing was the father of her baby. But the matter was not settled until June 2002 when Bing flew into London's Heathrow Airport and had a DNA test on the tarmac of the runway before turning tail and heading straight back to Los Angeles.

He needn't have bothered. By that time the first pictures of the baby had been published in the Press and one had only to look at them to know who Damian's father was. He was the spitting image of Steve Bing. The DNA test results bore this out and Elizabeth was vindicated. If not exactly a triumph, she could at least take comfort in the fact that she had been proved right. Her reputation was restored whereas Steve Bing was left looking like the worst kind of cad. The British Press, loyal to its own, described him as the biggest bounder since Diana, Princess of Wales's former lover James Hewitt.

Amid such bitterness and accusation, suffice it to say that Bing was not expected at Damian's christening. In keeping with his mother's glamorous lifestyle, the ceremony on July 6 was a star-studded affair. The 30 guests included Sir Elton John and his

partner David Furnish, David and Victoria Beckham, supermodel Elle Macpherson and actress Patsy Kensit. The names of
the six godfathers, far from being a list of old acquaintances or
childhood friends, read like a who's who of the rich and famous.
There was Elton John, arguably Britain's most successful pop
star and a Knight of the Realm to boot; his boyfriend David
Furnish, a film-maker who had become a close friend and
favourite walker of Elizabeth's; and aristocrat Henry Dent-
Brocklehurst, multi-millionaire owner of Sudeley Castle.

Hugh Grant, international film star and Elizabeth's former
lover of 13 years' standing, was also chosen although he did not
attend the ceremony. American actor Denis Leary, with whom
Liz had been linked romantically, was godfather number five
and last, but by no means least, was Teddy Forstmann, the 62-
year-old American billionaire financier and one of the richest
men in the world. Whatever else young Damian Hurley may
lack in his life, he will never be short of expensive gifts at
Christmas and on birthdays.

It came as a surprise to some that Elizabeth chose only men
for the role of godparent. After all, most women choose their
closest girlfriends or even their sisters for the important honour,
and in Elton John's case Liz had known him for only a short
amount of time. But to those who know her well, it came as no
surprise. 'Liz is not a girl's girl,' states someone who has met her
on many occasions. 'It is interesting that she had only godfathers
for the baby. The girl has no girlfriends. OK, she goes shopping
with Elle Macpherson in London – how superficial.'

It is certainly true that Elizabeth appears to prefer the
company of men to that of women. Explaining her decision to

choose all male godparents for Damian, she said: 'Otherwise it's like being in a harem smothered by big bosoms and wafting scents.' She had selected each one very carefully. 'Teddy can play golf with him, Henry can teach him to shoot, Hugh can take him to see Fulham play football, so we can dole it all out,' she continued.

As Elizabeth's choice of outfit for the christening day showed, she was not going to be a conventional mother in any sense of the word. Not for her a practical two-piece with pockets large enough to conceal the regulatory muslin square in case young Damian was sick. The sheer dress Liz chose had no room for even the tiniest scrap of tissue. And it was white that most impractical of colours for child-rearing. As every mother knows, babies and white are not a happy combination.

Yet in the months immediately following Damian's birth, Elizabeth was scarcely to be seen wearing any other colour. As well as the christening ensemble, there was the dramatic, plunging *haute couture* white dress in which she showed off her speedily regained figure during her first public engagement in July, and an enormous array of white camisoles and jumpers that she chose for everyday wear. As she carried her increasingly large baby around, the two of them would even wear matching white sheepskin jackets. But as an internationally renowned model, the practicalities of an outfit were probably the last thing on her mind. What mattered most to Elizabeth was how the clothes would make her look, and, more importantly, what message they would give out.

The connotations were obvious and it didn't take an Einstein to work out that in the aftermath of the humiliating Steve Bing slanging match, Liz was attempting to portray herself as whiter than white. White: the colour of snow; innocent; pure; unblemished; purified from sin. Virtually every time she was captured by a camera Liz looked exactly the same: clothed in white and clutching her infant to her breast. The woman who had set the pulses of millions of men racing with a hundred sexy outfits appeared to have been born again as a chaste earth mother and, more pertinently, vulnerable single mum.

'Elizabeth uses the language of clothes very cleverly,' says *Tatler* editor Jane Proctor. 'For instance when she's in a situation where she feels threatened she will retreat to jeans and a casual shirt which says, "I'm very wholesome." And she made her first appearance after the baby was born wearing an absolutely stunning white dress with a very, very low cut front that said: "I'm a mother, I'm still breastfeeding, but I'm still utterly gorgeous."'

It is a practice Elizabeth has honed to a fine art. 'When you monitor the clothes she has worn at key moments in her career, the white dress seems to be a favourite she comes back to,' says film critic Sean Macaulay. 'It is always the white dress and there's something quite funny about that body being cloaked in a virginal white. It creates a certain erotic tension which is very effective.'

But from the moment she stepped on to the red carpet on Hugh Grant's arm wearing 'That Dress' at the première of *Four Weddings and A Funeral*, Elizabeth has proved herself to be an expert at attracting attention. In the years since then, she has gone from being a struggling British actress to one of the most famous faces in the world. Rich in her own right, her glamorous lifestyle is a source of endless fascination to the public, both male and female. As her friend Birgit Cunningham puts it: 'When Liz walks into a room every man wants her and every girl is jealous of her. There is something about Liz in the same way there was something about Marilyn Monroe. When she walks into a room jaws drop.'

The media's obsession with Elizabeth Hurley is such that scarcely a day goes by without her appearing in a magazine or newspaper, filling the void left by the death of Diana, Princess of Wales. The two women have more than a little in common. Both were involved with high-profile partners whom they later eclipsed, and both became addicted to the lure of fame. 'Like Diana, she is a woman obsessed with the image reflected back at her from a thousand lenses,' *The Independent* newspaper said of Liz. Talking about her failed romance with Steve Bing, Elizabeth echoed the late Princess's famous remark about James Hewitt by saying: 'I adored him.'

Once described as being made of 'lip gloss and steel', Elizabeth is known to be a tough cookie and, dangerously for her enemies, a smart one too. Determined to find fame from a young age, she has achieved her goal, although not necessarily in the manner that she might have hoped. *Vogue* magazine called her 'a text-book example of how to be famous without being successful', and it is doubtful that her skills as an actress were ever going to be enough to propel her into the super league. Neither, in themselves, were her stunning looks and perfect figure. Instead it was her skills as a self-publicist, and an ability to walk the fine line between over-exposure combined with a natural instinct for exploiting the moment, that would make Elizabeth Hurley a household name.

2 Hurley Days

Her voice is pure cut glass and her vowels that of a 1930s duchess. It has become her trade mark, instantly recognizable and marking her out, particularly in America, as the classic English rose.

Elizabeth Hurley both looks and speaks the part of an upper-class girl from the Home Counties. But the image is an illusion. Weekends in country houses and expensive Swiss finishing schools were not on the agenda for the young Elizabeth. Her ancestors had been housemaids in such houses, and home for Liz Hurley was a modest bungalow in Buckskin, a district of Basingstoke new town. And far from being educated at a top public school, she attended a sprawling comprehensive along with twelve hundred other mainly working-class pupils.

But she was never going to be happy with the tag 'Liz Hurley Comprehensive Girl'. Feeling out of place in the suburban confines of Basingstoke and the Harriet Costello School, Elizabeth had a burning desire for more. And while the authentic upper middle-class girls from Roedean and Cheltenham Ladies' College were abandoning their posh accents in favour of the infinitely more cool estuary English,

Elizabeth was adopting a manner of speaking that came from a bygone age.

Despite what the Americans may like to think, the Queen's English as spoken by Elizabeth Hurley no longer really exists in modern Britain. The only people who actually speak that way today are an ever-dwindling number of octogenarian former debutantes – and Liz. Mimicking the accent of the upper classes of yesteryear was the young Elizabeth's first step to achieving her heartfelt need to be noticed. It was a successful ploy and her voice, combined with her already stunning good looks, ensured that she was the centre of attention from a young age.

She was born Elizabeth Jane Hurley on June 10, 1965, in Hampshire. Her father was at that time a captain in the Royal Army Educational Corps, and Elizabeth was born at the family home at number one Aisne Road, Blackdown, near the army barracks at Aldershot where her father was stationed.

Her dad Roy was an Essex man born and bred but his family roots lay several hundred miles away in Southern Ireland. His ancestors can be traced back more than a hundred and sixty years to a Mary Dixon, who was Elizabeth's great-great-grand-mother. Mary was born into a poor family and worked as a housemaid in County Cork. She married Charles Hurley, a boatman from Passage West, a small port six miles from Cork city, and shortly afterwards the couple emigrated to England. They had no doubt left Ireland hoping for a better life, but in the event they ended up swapping the disease-ridden Passage West for the depressing slums of East London. Charles found work in the capital as a decorator but was to die of exhaustion aged just forty-seven.

His son, Charles junior, also worked as a painter and once lodged at a boarding house in Stepney, near Jack the Ripper's notorious hunting ground. On Christmas Day, 1896, he married his next-door neighbour Ellen Maud Croucher, a 24-year-old housemaid. When their son was born a year later they named him Charles. Charles was to be a favourite Hurley name and over a hundred years later Elizabeth would honour the family tradition by giving her son the moniker too.

By the turn of the century, the Hurleys' fortunes had improved and they were able to escape the East End slums, with their eighty thousand prostitutes and high mortality rates, and set up home in a terraced house in Hackney overlooking a canal. The young Charles – Liz's grandfather – was educated and gained a position as a printer's clerk. Prospering nicely, he left East London for the new suburb of Forest Gate just outside London. In 1922, at the age of 24, he married printer's daughter Frances Annie Cook. His bride, a widow, was some six years older than him but coyly put her age on the wedding certificate as 26. Elizabeth's father was born seven years later, in 1929, by which time the family was living in Dagenham, Essex.

Roy Leonard Hurley joined the army when he left school and initially forsook marriage and children for an army career. However, part of his work for the Educational Corps involved attending a teacher training college in Hampshire and it was there that he met his future wife, a pretty music teacher called Angela Mary Titt. They were married in 1962 and immediately planned a family. Kathleen, their first child, was born in early 1964, followed 16 months later by Elizabeth. The arrival of a son, Michael, in 1969 completed their family.

Chapter 2

For the first 12 years of Elizabeth's life the family moved around a lot because of her father's job, but they eventually settled in Buckskin, a leafy suburb of Basingstoke, Hampshire. Her parents bought a detached bungalow in Buckskin Avenue and while it could hardly be described as palatial, it was the only house in the road to boast a swimming pool, albeit a rather small one.

Elizabeth's sister Kathleen, who is known as Kate, has said that even as a baby Liz was a determined attention-seeker. She recalls how the young Elizabeth would scream constantly for attention and would throw 'outrageous tantrums' if she was ignored. Until the age of eleven Elizabeth attended Kempshott Junior School, a local state school. Fellow pupils maintain that she stood out from the crowd even then. 'She was always the prettiest, you could tell from the way she held herself and her general demeanour that she was going to be someone,' says former classmate Elizabeth Harris. 'She was never outlandish, but you always knew she was there. She had a kind of presence about her.'

Liz decided that she wanted to be famous at the tender age of eight when she watched Marie Osmond singing 'Paper Roses' on *Top of the Pops*. The year was 1973 and the boys in her class at school all had crushes on the pretty American singer. Liz was later to admit that she was beside herself with jealousy. This was not because she had the hots for any of the boys herself, however. On the contrary, Elizabeth was not at that time interested in boys in a romantic sense at all, but she wanted them to be attracted to her because she wished to be the centre of attention. Her sister recalled how one particular boy used to skateboard outside their house and look wistfully up at the window, hoping that Elizabeth would come out. 'She kept herself to herself when it came to boys,' says Elizabeth Harris. 'There was quite a queue of lads who were interested in her but she never took much notice of them.'

This is not particularly unusual, given that Elizabeth was not yet a teenager, but by her own admission she would not become interested in the opposite sex until far later than her contemporaries. 'We were always forming all-girl gangs which were famous for electing boys as enemy number one,' she has said. 'I used to be fancied by an awful lot of boys, but I loathed them.' Fame was the lover that she ardently pursued, and there wasn't a boy in Basingstoke who could compete with its charms.

For many years Elizabeth was also far more interested in dancing than in boys and she had private ballet lessons for three hours a night after school. The Hurleys were not a stereotypical military family. 'Dad did all the cooking and mum changed the plugs,' Liz explained. But while having a teacher for a mother and an army major for a father could have made for a strict upbringing, the emphasis in Elizabeth's house was on tolerance rather than discipline. 'Some of my friends had horrid upbringings,' she said. 'I never did.' Although the family was comfortably off, they were by no means rich. Elizabeth has described her upbringing as 'fish fingers and peas for supper and holidays in Devon as opposed to Mustique'. But her parents managed to find the extra money needed to pay for her ballet lessons. 'My parents are marvellous, I absolutely worship them,' she said in 1991. 'They used to drive me miles to ballet and drama classes and wait for hours. It makes me cry when I think of it. My mother used to scrimp on buying things for herself to buy my tap shoes. They were brilliant.'

But Elizabeth's relationship with her mother was not one of pally friends who would go shopping together and share secrets. 'It wouldn't be really hard to freak my mum out,' she said in 2000. 'We have a very mother–daughter relationship. We're not friends, I like her to be very mummy-ish so I never discuss my boyfriends on any level with her. She would be shocked if I ever alluded to sex in any way, shape or form. She probably thinks I'm a virgin. I've never stayed with a boyfriend in her house.'

As well as her dedication to ballet, by the time she reached her teens Elizabeth was also heavily involved in amateur dramatics. As a young girl she had realized that a guaranteed way to get noticed was to stand on stage, and she would persuade her friends to put on plays with her and invite other army parents to come and watch. Determined to bring herself to a wider audience than simply performing in front of a few soldiers' families, at thirteen she joined the Basingstoke Amateur Theatrical Society. But there, as in her subsequent acting career, it was for her looks rather than her thespian talents that she was to stand out. 'Even at 13-and-a-half she was gorgeous,' recalls Aileen Scriven, who was one of the company. 'The backstage lads, who were all older than she was, were all ga-ga about her. They fell over themselves to be near her.'

But asked to recall if Elizabeth was actually any good in the society's productions, Mrs Scriven is more hesitant. 'It's so difficult to remember,' she says diplomatically. 'She looked good and she sounded good. She played her part well. You wouldn't say she walked on the stage as a natural star because she hadn't had any experience then.'

The first show in which Elizabeth appeared was *Hansel and Gretel*. Liz, naturally, was Gretel. And when she auditioned for *Jack and the Beanstalk* two years later, she did so in full ballet kit and easily secured the coveted role of pantomime fairy. 'Her dancing was very good and she just looked right,' says Aileen. 'She has got wonderful bone structure and she'll have that to the day she dies. Her mother's got it too. She also has a lovely voice. She's got a lot of natural attributes and I think she's actually done extremely well with what she's got. She's made the most of her assets, let's face it. And who can blame her.'

Aileen Scriven and the other members of the society may have recognized Elizabeth's beauty, but her own account of herself at that time was rather less flattering. 'I was under five foot when I was 15,' she has said. 'I had no boyfriends, I was the last girl to develop, to wear a bra, to kiss a boy.' Her lack of confidence in the way she looked was compounded by the fact that for much of her childhood she felt very much in her older sister's shadow. 'My sister was a towering beauty at age 10, while I was sort of this midget child,' she has stated. The close age gap between the two girls had meant that they were able to be friends as well as siblings. But as she grew older, Elizabeth's hitherto happy relationship with her sister became more complicated. The two had always been close, almost obsessively so, but as she watched her sister blossoming into a pretty teenager, Elizabeth began to feel jealous of Kate.

During a family holiday to Cornwall one summer, Elizabeth watched Kate being pursued by admiring suitors on the beach and felt furious. Her own still childish body clad in Laura Ashley clothes and her feet encased in T-bar sandals, she admits she was 'absolutely livid because no one would look at me'. The incident was to bring about a marked change in their relationship. A late developer, it would be some time before Elizabeth developed curves of her own but from then on she viewed Kate as someone to be competed with.

Elizabeth maintains that she hated her young teenage body, believing herself to be too thin. As someone who earns her living by wearing tiny clothes, she can surely be excused if she is nowadays somewhat obsessed with diet books. She claims to have read every one ever written and has plans to write her own. But although her interest in them started young, in those days she read them solely in an attempt to gain weight. She would swot up on all the latest fads and then carry out the instructions in reverse. 'I was painfully thin as a child,' she has said. 'When I was 14 I was still only four feet nine. All my friends were getting big and getting sexy and I still looked like I was six. So I would do pathetic things like stuff tissues in the back of my jeans to create a figure. When I was sixteen I started to look a bit more grown up. I shot up ten inches in a year, which was very weird. Still I looked very, very young for my age, which I hated.'

Elizabeth may have been the last girl in her class to need to wear a bra but she was the first to wear make-up. And in a portent of things to come, she discovered the advantages of having clothes specially tailored for her while still a schoolgirl. Lamenting her 'odd shape' – she has big shoulders and slim hips – shop-bought clothes never fitted her properly. 'Ever since I can remember, from school uniforms onwards, I have had to have everything "coutured" for me, albeit by my mum with her trusting Singer sewing machine from the 1960s,' she has recalled. It is no big surprise that clothes and the way they fitted were immensely important to her. She simply loved them and the more glamorous the better. Aged nine, she used to spend hours in needlework class trying to copy Marilyn Monroe's dresses. 'We always had the biggest dressing up box in our house with crowns, jewels, fake fur and stuff. I guess I have never grown out of it.'

When she left Kempshott Junior School at the age of 11, Elizabeth enrolled at the local comprehensive, Harriet Costello. There her inherent style and love of pretty things did not go unnoticed by the other girls, some of whom were envious of her nice possessions. It made her stand out for all the wrong reasons. 'She was teased because she came from a good family and she had nice clothes and nice shoes,' says fellow pupil Trudie Graves. 'Her hair was always nice, she always had make-up and a really nice school bag and a lot of people were jealous.'

Harriet Costello had been an all-girls school but by the time Liz joined in the late 1970s it was co-educational. And while she was the focus of envy from some of the girls, Elizabeth was drawing altogether far more favourable looks from the boys there. Those who were lucky enough to be in classrooms that looked on to the playing fields were in for a particular treat when it was time for Elizabeth to walk by in her games kit. 'We used to have maths lessons at the same time that the girls had PE and when the girls came in from games you'd see Liz walk up to the kerb, put her foot up and bend over to undo her hockey boots,' says former pupil Colin West. 'Everybody was just staring out of the window. She had an amazing figure and lovely legs.'

Away from school, Elizabeth was also on the receiving end of plenty of male attention. 'The thing that stood out about her was the way she looked,' says Aileen Scriven. 'The beautiful bone structure was there at 13 and she was very popular with all the young fellas in the chorus.' Elizabeth naturally lapped it up. 'She knew she was pretty and she knew that the boys flocked around her like a magnet,' recalls Aileen. 'She was aware of the effect she had on them, of course she was.'

Elizabeth has painted a picture of herself as a wilful schoolgirl rebel. She says that while her sister was neat and hard-working, she was scruffy and the bane of her teachers' lives. She also claims to have been thrown out of the Brownies and to have run away from school. But this too is part of the illusion. Aileen Scriven remembers an altogether more agreeable youngster than the one she describes. 'I would have been involved with chaperoning her because she was under 16 and I don't remember having any problems with her at all,' she says. 'She was very much still a schoolgirl. All girls are giggly and she was giggly with the rest but she was actually pretty quiet.'

This is a consensus shared by her teachers. 'She was in one of the top streams and she did well in her GCEs,' says Chris Fleming, who still teaches at Harriet Costello, where he is now the deputy head. 'She was noticeable but I don't remember her ever getting into trouble.' Elizabeth was especially good at English and she achieved grade A in both English language and English literature. She got a grade B in maths, geography and French, grade C in German and religious education and grade D for music. She was keen to continue her education, and, as Harriet Costello did not have a sixth-form facility, she enrolled at the nearby Queen Mary's College to do a one year A-level course in English, sociology and psychology.

At sixth-form college Elizabeth struck up a satisfying relationship with her English lecturer, Andrew Dickens. 'Elizabeth loved literature and was a delight to teach because she always engaged with the teacher,' he says. 'She loved reading plays and she had a real ear for the cadences of speech. She loved language.' It was at this time that Elizabeth first came across the novels of Evelyn Waugh and she and Andrew Dickens would spend hours animatedly discussing the books' merits. Elizabeth adored Waugh's darkly comic style and his brilliant use of language. Her particular favourite was *Vile Bodies*. Published in 1930, the book satirized the shallow, feckless world of the Bright Young Things of the Roaring Twenties. Featuring characters such as Fanny Throbbing, Creative Endeavour and Mrs Ape, and peppered with expressions like 'divine' and 'too sick-making', the book introduced Elizabeth to a whole new way of speaking.

She had always been well spoken, but she now exaggerated her voice and began to mimic the speech patterns of Waugh's characters. 'Elizabeth would often talk about people being "perfectly beastly" or "perfectly horrid",' says Dickens. 'I remember her writing to me once and saying, "College has stretched my tolerance." She had a tendency to speak that way anyway, but in Evelyn Waugh she found it written down. It was a code of language which, tongue in cheek, suited her perfectly.'

Some 10 years later, Elizabeth would take her mimicry of Waugh's characters to new heights when she moved to Los

Angeles and began actually to live the lifestyle of the 'Vile Bodies'. But in 1982 she was content with the effect that her new way of speaking had on her Basingstoke compatriots.

Elizabeth left school in the summer of 1981 as Lady Diana Spencer was preparing to walk down the aisle to marry Prince Charles. Britain was in the grip of Royal Wedding fever but while girls all over the country were enraptured by the frilly, romantic fashions inspired by Diana's wedding dress, Elizabeth was going for an altogether bolder look.

She still hungered desperately for attention and when her sister became a punk rocker Liz discovered a style of dressing that was guaranteed to have maximum impact. That Kate should have thought of it before her was a cause of some annoyance to Elizabeth and she has admitted that she was 'incredibly jealous' of her sister's eye-catching new look. Not one to be outdone, Liz decided that she too would become a punk rocker and determined to outshine her sister.

But there was one problem. Elizabeth had no idea how to go about transforming herself into a figure of anarchic rebellion and Kate, in all honesty, made for a rather tame punk rocker. However, help was at hand and when she and Kate attended a fancy-dress party in the local village hall one evening in 1982, Elizabeth met a girl who was to become a major influence on her.

Debra Holder was four years older than Elizabeth and had the distinction of being Basingstoke's first punk rocker. Sporting a black Mohican haircut and wearing a tiny miniskirt and fishnet tights, she turned heads wherever she went. Elizabeth took one look at her and was completely bowled over by the older girl's style. Liz, however, cut an altogether less glamorous figure that night, dressed as she was as the back end of a horse. By anyone's standards it was a bizarre, albeit eye-grabbing entrance.

But if Elizabeth was dazzled by the stunning punk girl with the partially shaved head, Debra thought Elizabeth equally impressive. 'Halfway through the party a pantomime horse walked in,' Debra recalls. 'All of a sudden the head was pulled off and I saw Katie. She was at the front, and Liz was the back. I just thought, "Wicked!" and started talking to her then and there.'

The two girls made a beeline for each other. 'We approached each other more or less at the same time,' says Debra. 'I walked over to her just as she came towards me. She told me that she wanted to get into punk and asked me how she should do her hair and what she should wear. I talked to her about fashion because she really wanted to know what sort of clothes to wear and where you could get stuff.' The girls talked all evening and by the time they left to go home they were firm friends. The next time they met Elizabeth was totally changed. 'Liz became a punk overnight,' says Debra. 'She was like a mad thing. I advised her about what to wear and she got things straight away. She had her ears pierced several times and wore big chandelier-type earrings all the way up her ears. She got a leather jacket with studs on and painted [Siouxsie and] the Banshees on it. And she had her nose pierced and wore a ring in it.'

To begin with Elizabeth unashamedly aped her new pal's style. 'She used to copy the way I dressed,' says Debra. 'If we were going out for the evening she would phone me up to find out what I was going to wear and she'd wear exactly the same.' But one thing Elizabeth wasn't about to copy was her friend's Mohican hairstyle. At the time she had extremely long hair that earned her admiring glances wherever she went. It was her crowning glory and she was immensely proud of it. 'Her hair was well past her bum and almost down to her knees,' says Debra. 'Everyone was attracted to her because of her hair being so long. It was unusual.' However, Liz later plucked up the courage to be a bit more daring and had half of it cut off. 'Because it was so long she couldn't make it stand on end so she cut the top to about 12 inches so she could spike it up,' says Debra. 'She would put the rest of it into lots of little plaits, or just one great big long plait at the back. It looked amazing.'

Emboldened by her attempts at do-it-yourself hairdressing, Liz decided to experiment with dyeing her hair. It was an unmitigated disaster. 'I told her to be careful,' says Debra. 'I thought she was just going to dye the top bit but she bleached it all over and it went bright orangey yellow. It looked awful, like straw, and it had kinky bits in it like cotton wool.' Undaunted, Liz simply put a hair colour over the top and dyed the whole lot bright pink. 'It looked a bit better but it was too much on that length of hair,' says her friend. 'So she dyed the majority of it black and just left the top part white and pink. Her hair was really thick – well, it was until she started bleaching it!'

By the time punk rock reached Basingstoke and was embraced by Elizabeth it was really on the way out. Its heyday had been in the late 1970s and by 1982 it was the frilly-shirted New Romantics who were all the rage. But catching the tail end of the punk movement suited Elizabeth because it meant that she could be a more feminine punk. 'She became a punk at the right time because punk had turned a bit nicer than the real hard line stuff,' explains Debra. As she gained in confidence Elizabeth stopped copying her friend's way of dressing and developed her own style. Unsurprisingly, it was one chosen with careful thought to the impact it would have on those around her.

'She used to make some good stuff,' says Debra. 'She wore beautiful ball gowns in bright shocking colours which she would rip to bits and put netting over the top. She had a lot of flair in the way she dressed. On one occasion we went to a party in a children's home in Basingstoke and whenever I walk past there now I remember Liz sitting in the garden. She was in a beautiful sherbet lemon ballgown and really high stiletto shoes, she was really tanned, and she had her black hair spiked out on top and in a long black plait to her waist. She looked really beautiful.'

While Elizabeth was much in awe of her street-savvy friend, Debra in turn admired the way that Liz stood out from the crowd. 'You could have put her anywhere in the country, in any town, and she would have been special,' she says. 'She stood out from all the rest. She had that look about her, she carried herself well and she had confidence. She was also a nice person and she had a willingness to join in with things and be friends. She was amazing. I said to her once that maybe she should pluck her eyebrows but she said no because she didn't want to look like everyone else.'

The punks' social life was centred around the Great Western pub in Basingstoke town centre. 'We'd meet up in the Western because the train station was right opposite and we could get the train to various gigs,' Debra explains. 'Liz was well known by the guards, she would talk to anybody. We used to play cards round the table with all the gang and drink pints of snakebite, made from lager and cider. We'd put shots of Pernod and black-currant in them too. It was really bad for your stomach but Liz used to put quite a lot of drink away on a good night. She handled it quite well. At weekends we would go down the park in the afternoon and drink cider. There would be a whole gang of us and we'd watch people go by and lie on the grass and have a bit of a playfight.'

There wasn't really much else for a bunch of renegade punks to do in boring Basingstoke and much of Liz's and Debra's time was spent planning trips to London. 'She liked Siouxsie and the Banshees and Bauhaus was her main thing,' says Debra. 'I was more into mad punk but she would come to all the gigs I wanted to go to, she didn't mind. They were mainly in London and we used to think London was great.'

Liz financed her new lifestyle with a series of part-time jobs, none of which she was very good at. 'I don't have a very good track record,' she has admitted. 'When I was a waitress I couldn't bear everybody being awful to me. Just because I wore a short skirt people assumed I was a dimwit. I was terribly impertinent back to them so I was sacked. After that I worked in a garden nursery and got sacked from there too. I overfed all the goldfish and they all died.' Elizabeth also tried doing telesales for a local double-glazing firm and had a Saturday job as an assistant in the Basingstoke department store Owen Owen. These jobs also ended badly for Elizabeth. 'I was sacked from the clothes shop for dyeing my hair pink and I was even sacked from selling double-glazing on the phone,' she has said. 'I did try to work hard but I wasn't very good at it.'

Fortunately for Elizabeth her mother and father would help

her out financially. 'Her parents were well off and they used to give her a few pounds,' says Debra. 'And she and another girl called Diane Claridge used to go up to London and busk in Covent Garden and Charing Cross station. They had a little battery-operated record player and they would do a tap-dancing routine. There weren't too many tap-dancing punks in London and I think they used to do really well out of it.' Liz was happy to share any money she made with her less well-off friends. 'She's a really generous person and she'd pay for people if they had no money,' says Debra.

Liz and her pals would sometimes go twice a week to the capital where they would spend the evening drinking in down-at-heel punk clubs. The highlight of these trips was deliberately missing the last train home in order to spend the night sleeping rough at Waterloo station. 'It was all terribly daring, having to miss the last train back so we could sleep at Waterloo station,' she has said. Her parents appear to have been remarkably laid back about their daughter staying out all night. 'All my friends used to be home at midnight but we never, ever had a going home time,' Liz has recalled. 'My parents always picked me and my sister up whenever we wanted them to.'

One of the reasons that Liz's parents were so tolerant was because they didn't know exactly what she was getting up to. They also mistakenly thought that she was with her older sister. 'She got to stay out at night because she and Katie would provide alibis for each other,' says Debra. 'Liz would say "I'm with Katie and her boyfriend", but if her parents had known they'd have gone mad. We used to spend the night anywhere we ended up. We'd get drunk and fall asleep in the clubs and when they kicked us out we'd stagger to the station and sleep there until the morning. We didn't care, we just roughed it. But Liz never hitch-hiked because she was quite concerned with her personal safety.'

It was at such times that Liz realized she was fortunate to have a sister she could be in cahoots with. 'Katie and Liz were always together,' says Debra. 'Katie was into Siouxie Sioux and so was Liz. Katie went round with a posher lot but they were very close.' But despite the sisters' undeniable closeness, Debra could tell straight away that Liz felt overshadowed by her older sibling. 'Katie had all the friends and it was obviously bugging Liz at the time because she was doing ballet and a lot of her time was spent studying rather than socializing,' she explains. 'When Liz did come out on the scene she relied on Katie for introductions. She felt in Katie's shadow because Katie was a very friendly, nice girl and she seemed to be the more powerful one at the time. But then Liz came out in her own way and overtook Katie.'

Part of the reason Elizabeth became a punk was so that she could dispel the goody-goody image she'd had at school. 'I had desperately wanted to be like other children at school but I never was,' she has said. 'I was teased like mad for the way I spoke so I tried to overcompensate for it by being very rebellious. It was an attitude that upset my parents horribly. I am certain that everyone does these silly, rebellious things from time to time, it's just that mine went on for a bit long.' Her friends noticed the difference in her behaviour after she left Harriet Costello. 'She certainly changed quite dramatically after leaving school,' says classmate Kathy Ledger. 'She was quite intelligent and good at school, but when she went to college and became a punk rocker I think she became less interested in her work.'

But Elizabeth was mindful not to be too rebellious or unruly. 'I was still sensible,' she has admitted. 'I went to college and I still went to drama classes.' And although she no longer performed in their productions, she still took an interest in the local amateur theatrical society. 'She had a mane of black hair and she used to come to the pantomimes and sit in the third or fourth row,' says Aileen Scriven. 'I used to think "Oh, Liz Hurley's in tonight" and I felt sorry for anyone sitting behind her because they couldn't have seen a thing!'

She may have dressed like Sid Vicious but in reality Elizabeth was more inspired by Evelyn Waugh. The dual influences were poles apart but Elizabeth managed successfully to combine them. She had transformed herself into a spiky-haired punk with pink hair and a nose ring but she continued to speak in an incredibly posh voice. In fact, if anything, her cut-glass accent became even more pronounced and her vocabulary more eccentric as she adopted the speech of Waugh's characters. 'I did think the way she spoke and the words she used was a bit unusual,' says Debra. 'It was very old-fashioned. I think it was quite contrived because her sister didn't speak like that.'

Elizabeth was living two very different lifestyles. She was taking three A-levels and still studiously attending ballet classes, but she was also hanging out in rough pubs and drinking pints of snakebite with her punk friends. She was careful to keep the different aspects of her life separate and would invite Debra and her friends round to her house only when her parents were out. 'I was never invited round when her parents were in, nobody was,' says Debra. 'I think Liz had a couple of sides to her. There was part of her that was about studying and knuckling down and going to private ballet lessons in Basingstoke. But she never talked about that sort of thing because that was her other life – her straight-laced life. And then there was the other side, which she lived as well in a full way, roughing it with the punks and going to rough gigs.'

Although Debra was her best friend, Elizabeth never introduced her to her parents. 'I never met Liz's mum but I got the impression she was really nice,' says Debra. 'She was fair and she used to let Liz get away with a lot. Liz did get on with her dad but he was very strict. He was a retired sergeant major. If I used to phone up and ask if Liz was in, he used to say, "It's Elizabeth to you." And then he'd listen in while we chatted.'

With her parents safely out of the way, Liz would invite her mates over to swim in the pool. On these occasions she ensured that she would be the centre of attention by sunbathing in front of the boys wearing only a pair of bikini bottoms. 'She used to be topless round the pool in the summer,' says Debra. 'She always had nice boobs. She had all the boys under her command. She's terribly bossy, in a nice way, and she used to dye the hairs on the boys' legs different crazy colours.'

When they weren't hanging out in the Western or going to gigs in London, Liz and Debra would hop on the train to Reading and go drinking. The Berkshire town was the nearest major nightspot to Basingstoke and Liz was a familiar face in the town. 'People were surprised when they heard this really posh voice come out of a punk, especially in Reading,' says Debra. 'We used to go there on alternate weekends, to a pub called The

Star. It was quite a well-known pub at the time and was full of punks. It was the roughest pub in town but it didn't faze Liz at all. She experienced all walks of life and because she had been well brought up she could speak to anybody.'

Elizabeth's habit of treating men as if they were little boys was to come in handy one night when the Western pub came under siege from a group of marauding skinheads. 'They'd come down from Reading and they let off a load of canisters in the pub,' recalls Debra. 'Me and Liz ended up in the loos covered in broken glass, Liz was literally shaking it out of her hair.' Elizabeth was furious at the skinheads' behaviour and gave them a tongue-lashing that reduced the hooligans to meek schoolboys. They had come armed for trouble but ended up looking and feeling extremely foolish as Liz let them have it with both barrels.

'We knew most of them and Elizabeth had a right go at them afterwards,' says Debra. 'She just berated them like a school-teacher. She said, "You're never coming to our pub again!" She has got a really vicious temper, but only with men usually. She went mad. When she's in a temper she has a tendency to give people an ear bashing and make them look really small. Even though she loses her temper she is still in control and because she's got a good command of the language people were afraid of starting her off because it would make them look stupid. The skinheads weren't scared of her but they did take notice. A lot of them fancied her and they were just in awe.'

Elizabeth acknowledges that she has a 'don't fool with me' voice. 'I suppose it is true, but I don't know why,' she has said. 'Maybe it's because I can't suffer fools at all. I can't stand rudeness.' But while she had little difficulty winning over men, Elizabeth had to work that bit harder in order to impress their girlfriends. 'When we went to other towns where she wasn't really known she did get a bit of aggro,' says Debra. 'Some of the girls turned against her but she could always turn the situation around and in the end people liked her. If girls were being bitchy to her she would be nice to them. She'd say something like, "Your jacket is absolutely gorgeous, where did you get it?" and she'd be friendly. Not in an over-the-top way, but she'd just be really nice and she used to win people over. She always used to say to me, "Oh, you look wonderful today," and she'd really mean it. She's a right charmer.'

Displaying a diplomacy way beyond her years, Elizabeth also made a point of studiously ignoring the boys until she had made friends with the girls. 'She would always check out the girls first because she wanted to make sure the ground was clear,' explains her friend. 'She knew that if she spoke to a boy first or was approached by a boy from a different town, the other girls would feel threatened so she always talked to them first. It was just her natural way. But she did attract attention from the boys – she couldn't help it. She didn't want to attract their attention so she could go to bed with them. She just liked the attention. It made her feel good.'

When she left St Mary's College after her A-levels, Elizabeth transferred to Basingstoke Technical College to continue her studies. But by that time her mind was more on having a good time than anything academic. She became entertainments officer of the student union and quickly became the centre of attention. 'She was top dog at the student union,' recalls former student Geraldine Wesolowski. 'She organized coach trips for us to see stuff like Gary Glitter, Siouxsie and the Banshees and Tenpole Tudor.'

Being naturally bossy, officialdom suited Elizabeth. 'Organizing things at the student union was right up her street,' says friend Derek Thompson. 'She was quite a strong personality and while she was by no means the ringleader she was good fun.' Liz also edited the college newsletter with her sister Kate, and Derek Thompson still remembers one particular article that she wrote. 'She did an article in which she basically slagged off the whole fashion industry.' He smiles. 'It was called "Stereotype" and all the material in it was taken from Germaine Greer's book *The Female Eunuch*. She used what Greer had written to really slate the fashion industry. It's funny because she was basically slagging off what she later became.'

Elizabeth was a big fan of the sexy dance troupe Hot Gossip and while watching them perform on TV on the *Kenny Everett Television Show* she came up with an idea to guarantee even more attention for herself. Together with Diane Claridge, whom she met at the Basingstoke Amateur Theatrical Society, and Bernadette Hunt, who had been a fellow student at St Mary's College, Elizabeth formed a raunchy dance act called the Vestal Virgins. Provocatively dressed in stockings and suspenders and thigh-high boots, the girls' stage act drove the boys wild. And carrying a huge dominatrix whip, which she would crack aggressively as she wiggled and strutted her way across the stage, Elizabeth was a major sensation.

'The skinheads and punks would surge onto the stage and she'd flick the whip at them and snarl, "Get back, boys!"' laughs

Debra. 'I lent her my thigh boots for the Vestal Virgins because she wasn't allowed to wear things like that. She was just about getting away with her punk look at home but she'd take her make-up with her and vamp it up more when she went out.'

Sadly for Liz, the Vestal Virgins were never going to be a rival to Hot Gossip and their reign in Basingstoke was pitifully short-lived. 'We weren't together very long as a group,' says Bernadette, who was later to find fleeting fame as Falcon in the television series *Gladiators*. 'We only really did one show and that was at the Basingstoke Tech College. Liz was out to shock everyone. She liked to be noticed.' But Diane Claridge recalls how, despite the efforts she went to in order to attract attention, Elizabeth seemed remarkably unfazed by the effect that she had on men. 'Liz was too involved with her dancing to be interested in boys who, even then, were drooling over her,' she says.

Elizabeth has put forward a rather surprising explanation for why she became a punk rocker. 'I think so many men took an interest that I wanted to make myself look as ghastly as possible so no one would whistle any more,' she said. 'It certainly stopped all the dirty old men leching after us. I think it is very tough for teenage girls when they look sexy before they feel sexy. It's very difficult.'

Yet if it was really her intention to stop men from wolf-whistling it seems odd that she should go to such lengths to gain their attention. And her best friend's recollections of Elizabeth's behaviour at the time simply do not bear this out. As well as sunbathing topless and cavorting on stage in stockings and suspenders, Elizabeth shunned underwear. 'Liz never wore knickers, even when she wore little leather miniskirts,' reveals

Debra. 'She was an exhibitionist. She'd get drunk later on in the evening and start crawling across the floor at some party and forget that it was all showing. Luckily it was usually quite dark so it was shadowed.' Hardly the conduct of someone who didn't want men to look at her but Elizabeth managed to get away with it. 'You would think that sort of behaviour would make people say that she was a slut,' says Debra. 'But no one ever did because she wasn't. They really respected her. All the blokes did.'

The main reason for this was that for a long time Liz didn't even date boys, much less sleep with them. She was a late developer in that respect and had been put off by a disastrous incident as a youngster. 'There was a boy in my chemistry class who I used to share lingering looks over the Bunsen burner with,' she once revealed. 'Then we finally kissed and I was repelled and repulsed. I didn't kiss anyone for three years after that.' This presumably wasn't one Phillip Simmonds, a former classmate at Harriet Costello Comprehensive about whom Liz was rather more kind. She even afforded him the title of first boyfriend although they were just thirteen at the time and it was all touchingly innocent. 'We went to see *Watership Down* together and snogged all the way through it,' she has recalled. 'I actually wanted to see the film. Every time I hear the song "Bright Eyes" I think of him.'

But despite her sexy figure and provocative way of dressing, Liz did not have a proper boyfriend until she was seventeen. The first boy she went out with was a fellow punk who went by the rather glorious name of Septic. He had also dated Debra and the two girls used to giggle about rumours they had heard concerning the size of his manhood. Neither of them was ever to discover if the rumours were true, however, as Debra claims they were both too scared to find out. Septic's real name was Antony Allcock and suffice it to say that he was supposed to live up to his name. Four years older than Liz and the same age as Debra, he modelled himself on singer Billy Idol and had spiky dyed blond hair and several earrings.

'Liz and I both went out with Septic, we used to share him,' says Debra. 'We thought he was the best-looking boy in Hampshire. He was well over six feet tall and gorgeous looking and he had all the girls chasing after him. I'd met him at a Stiff Little Fingers gig in 1978 but he later got into Sigue Sigue Sputnik and wore red rubber trousers and funny boots. He looked really good. I introduced him to Liz and they looked a perfect couple because they were both really tall and had lovely cheekbones.'

Antony Allcock recalls being completely bowled over by the 17-year-old Elizabeth. 'I met Liz in 1982 at the Fleet Country Club,' he says, talking for the first time about their relationship. 'It was a night club the rest of the week but on Wednesday evenings they used to have an alternative night, punk or heavy metal. I was going out with Debbie Holder and she introduced me to Liz. I thought, "Blimey, that's not bad, is it?" She was very good-looking. My first impression of her was, "Nice legs." She had a short skirt on and the visuals were very, very good.

'I just said hello and asked her if she wanted a drink. She used to drink snakebite and, as I later discovered, she could really knock it back. She enjoyed a drink but although there were drugs on the scene she was never into them. I asked her if she fancied meeting up again and she said yes. So we swapped phone numbers, as you do, and it went from there.'

Apart from Liz's lovely legs, Antony was extremely impressed by the way she spoke. 'One thing I liked about her, something that I found very endearing, is that she did speak differently to everybody else,' he says. 'Not only did she look good, but she had this voice that I found really rather nice. She had a talent for getting noticed and the voice was all part of that. Her sister didn't speak like that. In fact, you wouldn't believe they were sisters.'

But not everybody found Liz's upper-class accent such a turn-on. 'A lot of people used to take the piss out of her for the way she spoke,' he says. 'She handled it very well because she knew she was the best fucking biscuit on the scene basically. We'd go into a pub and when she opened her mouth some people would tease her. But she was still the best-looking girl in there, so why should she care?'

Antony enjoyed the attention that being seen with Elizabeth brought him. 'We attracted quite a lot of looks when we went out and it felt good,' he says. 'But there was a lot of jealousy from other girls. Liz liked the attention and I had heard a few things bandied about that she was an exhibitionist, but she never eyed up other guys when she was with me. With the right person she can be very loyal.'

While Elizabeth's punk friends were in awe of her parents, whom most of them never got to meet, she did take Septic home. 'I met her parents and they were fine,' he says. 'There was no problem at all. They took me being a punk as par for the course. Her dad never told me to get my hair cut or anything like that. Why should he? I wasn't in the army and neither was he by that time. They were very friendly.' The reason that Elizabeth's parents didn't object to their daughter dating Antony Allcock was because his wild image belied his altogether far more staid background. 'Septic wasn't a seedy character or anything,' says Debra. 'His mum was a nurse and he was a bit of a mummy's boy really. Instead of saying cake he'd say sponge.'

Liz and Septic would hang around in Basingstoke town centre with other youths and drink cider. They would also go to parties at friends' houses and punk concerts in London. But the date that sticks out most in Antony's memory was when he and Liz went to see The Damned in London. 'It was Christmas 1982 and when we got to Waterloo all the trains had gone,' he recalls. 'The only train left was going to Woking, so we went to Woking. We spent half the night on the train in Woking and the rest of it in the waiting room. We were sitting there while the shuntings were going back and forth and the workmen came and went. That was quite a night but Liz wasn't panicking about it, far from it. She was enjoying herself.'

Although Elizabeth was happy to go to concerts and hang around in noisy pubs, Antony could tell that being a punk didn't mean as much to her as it did to him. 'Liz wasn't really a punk, she just liked the dressing up and the theatrical side of it,' he says. 'I loved every minute of it but she just liked the image. In reality she preferred doing her singing and dancing and all that sort of cobblers. And she was probably very good at it. She knew that she didn't want to hang around with people with weird hair and all that kind of crap for ever. It was just a stage she was going through.'

Fellow punk Adrian Deevoy, who was then a member of local punk band Junk Factory, also suspected that Liz was simply playing at being a rebel. 'In a room full of people who fully expected to become superstars as a matter of course, she exuded an air of determined achievement,' he says. 'She had a plan. She studied ballet, she read books, she spoke about having a career with a passion that others reserved for planning a second nose ring. And she showed only a fleeting interest in cider consumption. That, in Basingstoke, was classy.'

Antony admits that he knew deep down that his relationship with Liz was not going to lead anywhere. He says, 'She had a kind of long-term grand plan, I suppose, and I always knew that it wouldn't include me. It didn't really bother me at the time because I was young then, but I think in her mind she always knew she was destined for better things. She never talked to me about her ambitions, I just had a gut feeling that she wanted more than she had. I fancied her and I thought she probably fancied me but it wasn't a heavy thing.'

However, the couple were to date for a whole year and when Elizabeth finally invited her boyfriend up to her bedroom he thought that his luck was in. There he was, standing in the inner sanctum of the girl whom half the boys in Basingstoke wanted to sleep with. But his joy at being there was to be frustratingly short-lived. As they kissed and cuddled on the bed he noticed a framed photograph of another man on the bedside table. And it wasn't that of another spotty-faced punk or local student either; it was of a handsome marine standing on board his ship as it sailed proudly into the Falklands. He asked Elizabeth who the man was and she told him it was Thomas Arklie. Seeing the look on her face as she mentioned Arklie's name, Antony realized that he and Liz had probably come to the end of the road. 'She already knew him when I knew her because she showed me a photograph of him,' he says.

Most men would have been gutted to see a photograph of another man lying next to their girlfriend's bed, but Septic claims to have taken it in his stride. 'I know it sounds weird, but I wasn't that pissed off about it,' he says. 'Liz and I liked each other but it wasn't a really serious type of thing.' He remains discreetly tight-lipped about what went on during his trips to her boudoir but says that they didn't have full sex. 'Liz was very tactile but I never slept with her,' he says.

Elizabeth was saving herself for the right man and that man was Thomas Arklie. They met in a Basingstoke pub when she was 17 and he was 23. 'I had just come back from the Falklands and must have been quite a catch,' says Arklie. 'We spent the night snogging in the pub with a pint of lager each, then kissed in the car until the sun came up.' But despite her passion for the hunky marine, Liz didn't immediately break off her romance with Septic. It suited her to have two guys interested in her and she wasn't about to put one of them off. 'She strung us both along,' admits Antony, who has given up punk and now works as a landscape gardener. 'She probably played us off against each other. Liz never liked to finish with anybody because she liked all the attention. Our relationship just fizzled out in the end. There was no big scene, we just stopped seeing each other. I stayed friends with her when she started going out with Tommy but the last time I saw her was in 1985. She had moved to London by then because she wanted to get into acting. I spoke to her once on the phone after that and that was it. Then about three years later I saw her on TV and thought, "Bloody hell!"'

Septic may have been Liz's first proper boyfriend, but Thomas Arklie was the man she first fell in love with. His handsome good looks and reputation as something of a local hero because of being in the Falklands were an irresistible combination as far as Elizabeth was concerned. 'Liz and Tommy were mad about each other,' says Debra Holder. 'He was really nice. He was very tall and muscly and fit-looking with jet black hair. Liz still came to the pub with the rest of us but rather than sit with the whole gang she would canoodle in the corner with Tommy. They were all over each other, really lovey-dovey. Even after a couple of years of going together they were like that.'

But although she was in love with Thomas Arklie, Elizabeth took her time before deciding to sleep with him. 'She was still a virgin then,' says Debra. 'It was well known. People would say, "Look at Liz, look how beautiful she is." The boys used to be mesmerized.' For his part, Arklie had fallen heavily for Elizabeth. 'I was in love,' he admits. 'I found her very attractive but I think it was quite a few weeks before we actually had sex.' The fact that Liz now had a steady boyfriend only served to make the other guys even more enamoured with her. 'They used to say, "God, Liz is so beautiful, she could have any man she liked, but she's only ever slept with one person,"' reveals Debra. 'They all used to look at her and think she was great and respect her."'

Liz introduced Thomas to her parents but his relationship with her mother and father was not a close one. 'I don't think he was round at her house all the time,' says Debra. 'I think he was invited to dinner now and again. Liz and Tommy were from very different backgrounds. Tommy's family are nice people but they are not from the same background as Liz's family.' However, the difference in their respective backgrounds did not stop Elizabeth from viewing Thomas Arklie as the man she would eventually marry. 'Liz was really serious about Tommy,' says Debra. 'It was a marriage job at the time. She's a very faithful type of person to her boyfriends, she was not a predator, ever.'

But by 1983 Elizabeth had had enough of boring Basingstoke and was about to head for London. And while her romance with Arklie would continue for some time to come, it was ultimately to become the first casualty of her relentless quest for fame.

3 Hugh's That Boy?

Liz was desperate to escape her unexciting home town – known as Doughnut City for its plethora of roundabouts – and swap suburbia for the metropolis. 'Living in a suburb of Basingstoke is hell for teenagers,' she has explained. 'All the talk was "When I move to London" but no one ever did.'

But typical of Liz, while others were content to dream their pipe dreams, she went and did it. Her sister Kate was keen to move to London too and for a while the sisters shared a flat. However, if Elizabeth had thought life in the capital would be glamorous, she was disappointed. Home was a humble bedsit in a rough part of Finsbury Park, North London. It had a broken window and a door that didn't lock properly but Liz knew no fear. 'I would walk home alone from pubs or clubs late at night without a thought of any danger,' she said. 'I had no trouble, though, and the only reason I can think of is that I looked so horrible in those days that no one would come near me.'

Elizabeth, at that stage, was still very much into the punk look. 'My hair was white, piled high, and looked rather frightening,' she says. 'It was sexy, but not page three sexy.' Her ambition had been to become a dancer with Hot Gossip on the

Kenny Everett Television Show but it was something she never achieved. The women who danced in Hot Gossip were experienced professional dancers, whereas Elizabeth didn't even have an Equity card. Without that crucial membership of the then compulsory actors' union she had to content herself with dancing five nights a week in an amateur troupe that she formed herself. Called Bodyline, the group performed at Roxanne's, a club in South Kensington, where Liz and the other dancers would gyrate to bands like The Clash. Being in the troupe had the advantage of enabling Elizabeth to gain the essential Equity card but it was not a happy time for her. Speaking a few years later when she had begun to find success as an actress she said, 'It breaks my heart to look back on that time.'

Life in London, where she knew hardly anyone, could be very isolating and at times she even found herself feeling homesick for boring old Basingstoke. 'She used to write and ask me to visit her because she was very lonely,' says her friend Debra Holder. Liz also missed her boyfriend because while she was attempting to forge a career for herself in London, Thomas Arklie was two hundred miles away at the marines' base in Plymouth. He would travel up to see her at weekends, where Liz would take him to punk clubs around Carnaby Street, but the rest of the time she missed him terribly. 'Tommy was away a lot with the marines and Liz didn't like that,' reveals Debra. 'They loved each other so much, they were besotted with each other. She often talked about marriage. She and Tommy were definitely going to get married and I think they did get engaged. They were perfect for each other.'

But shortly after she moved to London, Elizabeth had a

deeply upsetting experience while she was out with Thomas. The couple had gone into a pub on the Kilburn High Road in search of a drink and some lunch. What happened next was to leave her feeling totally distraught and in floods of tears. It was summer, and she was wearing pink shorts and a little crop top. As was often her wont, Liz wasn't wearing underwear. As she and Tommy were standing at the bar waiting to get served, a man came up behind Liz and pulled her shorts down, exposing her to the entire pub.

As well as being extremely cruel, it was not perhaps the wisest thing to do to a girl whose boyfriend just happened to be a marine. But as Thomas Arklie stepped in to protect her it was clear that he was hopelessly outnumbered. There was a scuffle and, incredibly, it was Liz and Thomas who were asked to leave. Liz was left shaken and traumatized by the experience and wrote an emotional letter to her friend Debra in which she poured out her heart. 'She was really upset,' says Debra. 'She said it was the worst thing that had ever happened to her. It humiliated her so much. Can you imagine how she felt to have that happen to her in a bar, in front of all those men? She couldn't believe that it had happened. How could they do that to her? She was probably the first pretty girl they'd ever seen in there because it was full of old men and old ladies drinking stout. Tommy went mad but the pub was packed so there was not a lot he could do. He was always very protective of her but he was outnumbered.'

Still keen on pursuing a career as a dancer, in 1984 the 19-year-old Elizabeth enrolled at the London Studios Centre, a dance school in King's Cross. Although she later described the centre as 'dreadful' and would ultimately be expelled, it was there that she really developed an interest in acting. The school also offered drama classes and Elizabeth struck up a good relationship with her drama tutor Ian Dewar. He remembers her as an eccentric student but was instantly impressed by her commitment and determination. To Elizabeth's surprise, Dewar singled her out for comic roles and he says people still talk about her comic performance as Sally Bowles in the college production of *Cabaret*. He admits he would like to see her exploit her talent as a comedienne. 'But she hates it,' he says sadly. It may be a sphere of acting that Elizabeth professes to dislike, but some critics believe that it is the one form of acting she is actually any good at. It is no coincidence that the role for which she received most plaudits was as Vanessa Kensington in the original Austin Powers film.

But Elizabeth never finished the three-year course. 'I left under a cloud,' she admitted. 'I was expelled, actually. I was spoilt rotten in my first two years and then I sort of just went out of favour. I went on holiday to a Greek island mid-term and didn't realize until I was on the plane that I had forgotten to tell them. I also missed the plane back. On returning, I was told to go to see the principal. She told me never to darken her doorstep again. So I said, "All right then," and minced off. The place was full of goody-goody ballet dancers anyway.'

And when Elizabeth later paid tribute to her teachers she made one pointed exception. 'I was very lucky in having terrific drama and English teachers when I was young who helped me enormously,' she said in an interview. 'But I had one rotten teacher and I got to see a confidential report she had written about me. It was three pages of pure venom. I had never read anything so nasty in my life. She said I was talentless, vain and the most dreadful child she had ever had to teach and didn't have a chance of succeeding in acting. It hurt me a lot but probably spurred me on to prove her wrong.'

Elizabeth wasn't down for long. Just a week after being expelled she landed a plum job touring the Middle East in a farce. It was 1986 and the late actor Derek Nimmo was organizing a tour of *The Man Most Likely To*. Veteran actor Leslie Phillips was to be Elizabeth's co-star and Nimmo later recalled how the two men were left poleaxed by the 21-year-old Elizabeth. 'This extraordinary creature arrived exuding sexual magnetism,' he said. 'As she left at the end of her audition, Leslie turned to me and muttered, "For Christ's sake." I gasped, "Good grief." And then we both realized that we had paid no heed to her acting ability. She was just so beautiful. We decided to audition her again at the Shaftesbury Theatre, where we would be a cricket pitch away from her and immune from her charms. She walked into the job.'

It was a wonderful opportunity and Elizabeth adored being on tour. 'I started work at nine o clock each night and after the performance there was a champagne reception,' she explained. 'I put on my best dress and went to be flattered. Then you were invited to do things like water ski the next day. There I was, in the very best locations, aged 21, being fed and fêted like a princess. I thought, "I could get used to this." It was purely being in the right place at the right time with the right people.'

Elizabeth's role involved lying on a chaise longue in a bikini and 'snogging' Leslie Phillips. It was a far from unpleasant experience for Phillips but he recalls how Elizabeth's penchant for shedding her clothes caused problems when they were staying in the ultra-conservative United Arab Emirates. 'In Abu Dhabi we almost had an international incident,' he says. 'She went swimming with some of the cast in a quiet little cove – topless. The police came down and were going to arrest her.' The crew had to do some quick talking to persuade them not to charge Elizabeth with breaking the strict local laws and she had to undertake to keep her top on in future.

The Middle East is famous for its ultra-luxurious hotels and the tour gave Elizabeth a taste for extravagant hotels which, she said, 'ruined my character for ever'. But somehow, no matter how fabulous the rooms, Elizabeth's always seemed to resemble a bombsite. The rest of the cast could not understand how such a pretty, well-spoken girl could be so horribly messy, but her sister has said Elizabeth is incapable of tidiness. 'She will leave a trail of havoc wherever she goes.' Elizabeth's own description of her dressing table at home bears this out. 'It is covered in receipts I'm saving for my accountant, broken earrings, books, half-full glasses of wine and old cups of tea,' she said in an interview. 'I am hideously untidy, I can't help it.'

Elizabeth was still in touch with Andrew Dickens, her teacher from St Mary's College in Basingstoke, and she wrote him gushing letters about the brilliant time she was having. 'I remember her writing to me from the Middle East when she was touring over there and saying, "I can't believe I'm actually here. All those places you told me about, I'm here,"' he recalls. Dickens says he was not surprised to hear her news as he had always known that she would go far.

By the time Derek Nimmo hired her for the overseas tour, Liz had successfully reinvented herself once again. As soon as she had decided that she really wanted to be an actress, not a dancer, she dumped the punk image as quickly as she had adopted it. 'I came to my senses and realized that I was not going to get any work unless I took out the nose ring and dyed my hair back to brown,' she explained. The new-look Elizabeth was much more sedate and owed more to the upper-class girls from Kensington and Chelsea than to her previous heroine Siouxie Sioux. 'She became a twin set and pearls kind of girl,' says Thomas Arklie. 'Much more Sloaney. She started to grow up.' But Elizabeth's big regret from her punk days was refusing her mother's bribe to get rid of the nose ring. 'She said that if I didn't take my nose ring out I couldn't have driving lessons,' she said. 'Of course after that I couldn't possibly take it out. So I can't drive.'

Around this time she also told her friends that she no longer wanted to be known as Liz. Henceforth, she said, she wanted to be called Elizabeth. Some of them were bemused by this new development. 'She didn't mind being called Liz at the time but I think that when she wanted to go into the limelight she wanted to come across as some sort of posh historical character,' says Debra Holder. And as she became more sophisticated, Elizabeth decided that she wanted a boyfriend to match. Like some sort of female Professor Higgins, she set about turning Thomas Arklie into a new man, coaching away his cockney accent and educating him about the finer things in life. 'I think she was a little embarrassed about my accent,' he says. 'I talked quite cockney but Liz changed my voice. She would correct my grammar, telling me off for using double negatives.'

Not every man would take kindly to having his speech corrected but not all of Elizabeth's bossy instructions were unwelcome. 'She opened my eyes to a lot of things,' Arklie admits. 'The first time I went to the theatre was with Liz. She would teach me new things all the time. She loved Evelyn Waugh and would give me books to read.' Elizabeth had always hated being separated from Thomas and eventually he gave in to her pleas and left the marines. 'She didn't like the idea of killing and gradually talked me out of it,' he says. Elizabeth's idea was that her good-looking boyfriend should try his hand at modelling. He agreed to give it a go and subsequently did a well-known TV advert for Carling Black Label in which he took off his clothes in a launderette. Arklie enjoyed making the ad and decided to try his hand at acting as well. But although it had been her idea for him to quit the marines, Elizabeth didn't like it when he expressed an interest in joining her world. She reacted indignantly when he dared to compare his television commercial work to her acting and his career change led to a series of clashes between them. Eventually their once loving relationship began to be destroyed by her jealousy.

'She crushed me in a sense,' he says. 'She'd say, "No, it's not acting you are doing, it's only modelling." I guess the continuing rows were why we split up. I couldn't get into acting while I was with Liz without it upsetting the status quo. She is quite overpowering and she became jealous.' Other people had noticed the tension between the couple as well. 'She did boss Tommy around,' says Debra Holder. 'She wanted him to do things her way. She thought he could better himself if he took her advice. But he rebelled against her. I could tell that she was upset about things. She would be very down and she'd say, "I've got nothing to look forward to, I'm fed up with London, I want to come back." But she kept going.'

Finally tiring of her jealous temper tantrums, Arklie decided to end the relationship. Used to being in control, Elizabeth did not take kindly to being jilted. 'Usually she's the boss in the relationship but she wasn't with Tommy,' says Debra. 'He commanded it in his own quiet way, and he finished the relationship. She was very upset because they were going to get married.'

But as Elizabeth was nursing a broken heart over Thomas Arklie, she was about to meet his replacement. In May 1987 she went for a part in a low-budget Spanish film about Lord Byron. The film was *Rowing in the Wind* and Elizabeth was up for the role of Claire Claremont, one of the poet's many mistresses. An up-and-coming English actor called Hugh Grant was in the frame to play Byron. The couple met during an introductory dinner with the director Gonzalo Suarez and Hugh later remarked that any reservations he had about appearing in a 'Europudding' movie evaporated the minute he laid eyes on Elizabeth. 'At the time I had an offer to do a serious BBC project and I couldn't decide between that and this absurd, career-damaging Spanish thing,' he explained. 'Then I saw Elizabeth and went for the absurd Spanish film.'

There was a good on-screen chemistry between the couple, although it was to be the first and only time that they would appear together in a film. Little wonder that they looked so comfortable in the bedroom scenes – in which Elizabeth appeared topless – for by that time they were lovers off-screen too. 'We were snogging on set and soon snogging off it too,' said

Elizabeth. 'I think it's really naff when actors and actresses go off
with one another, but we are very similar and just clicked right
away really.' She wrote to Andrew Dickens, enthusing about her
handsome co-star. 'I remember her saying, "I have the most
terrible crush on Lord Byron,"' says Dickens. 'She said he was
"cute" and "perfectly sweet".'

Grant was five years older than Elizabeth and already being
tipped as a big star. He had just starred in *Maurice*, the Merchant-
Ivory adaptation of E. M. Forster's novel about gay love. He was
clearly going places and Elizabeth wanted to go there too. The
two of them were to form a dynamic partnership, both person-
ally and professionally, and movie critic Karen Krizanovich later
described Liz meeting Hugh Grant as 'an act of God – if God was
her PR agent.'

Although he came from a similarly modest background to
Elizabeth, Hugh Grant shared her fascination with the English
upper classes. Born in London on September 9, 1960, Hugh John
Mungo Grant was the second son of James Grant, a former army
officer turned carpet salesman, and his teacher wife Fynvola. But
despite being brought up with his brother James in the thoroughly middle-class enclave of Chiswick, the young Hugh had
adopted faux aristocratic mannerisms and an eccentric way of
speaking. And while the punk rock movement had been and
gone with him barely noticing, he had Elizabeth's enthusiasm
for reading old childhood annuals and the writings of society
satirists such as P. G. Wodehouse.

He also shared her desire to throw off her boring roots and
create a more enigmatic persona for herself. But Hugh Grant had
been significantly more successful at turning himself into the

epitome of aristocratic English youth. While Elizabeth had attended the modest Harriet Costello Comprehensive, he had been educated at Godolphin and Latymer School, one of London's leading schools. And while she was completing her education in the decidedly unglamorous environs of Basingstoke Technical College, Hugh Grant was reading English at New College, Oxford. Throughout her teens and early twenties Elizabeth had to be content merely to speak in the manner of Evelyn Waugh characters, but at Oxford University Hugh Grant was able to take his admiration of the upper-class English lifestyle of yesteryear to new heights. Oxford was his ticket to the privileged way of life enjoyed by the character of Charles Ryder in Waugh's novel *Brideshead Revisited*, and Hugh threw himself wholeheartedly into emulating that long-gone lifestyle.

He threw lavish tea parties at his rooms overlooking the quad and he and his chums formed a drinking group, which they pretentiously named the Boojums Society from a reference in a Lewis Carroll book. He attended Keats Society meetings, the main features of which were apparently not earnest discussions about the learned poet, but drinking, eating and getting off with one's fellow students. There was also the Vile Bodies Club, named after the Evelyn Waugh book, which teddy-bear-toting undergraduates would attend, ludicrously dressed as Waugh characters.

All of this was to form a big part of Hugh's attraction for Elizabeth. As well as being attracted to the handsome floppy-haired actor in his tight breeches and his frilly Lord Byron shirt, Liz was hugely impressed by the fact that he had been to Oxford and lived the life of her literary heroes. 'Hugh is very clever and a clever man is hard to find,' she later remarked. To her mind, an Oxford graduate was a far more suitable proposition as a boyfriend for the new-look Elizabeth Hurley than a working-class ex-marine. 'Tommy was a nice bloke,' says Debra Holder. 'He was quiet but he knew how to behave and he carried himself well. But he looked like he knew more than he did.'

At Oxford, Hugh Grant had gone to great lengths to avoid the university's acting clique and despite his subsequent success he liked to give the impression that he considered acting to be rather ridiculous. 'He doesn't know what he's doing acting,' Elizabeth said not long after they met. 'He went to Oxford and is terribly bright and was going to be a writer. But people kept offering him parts and it was so much money he couldn't turn it down.' And whereas Liz had previously been very serious about her career, she now appeared to share his disdain. 'I think acting is a bit of a joke profession, quite honestly,' she said. 'I cannot take it really seriously.'

When she began dating Hugh Grant, Elizabeth fell in with a new crowd of friends, most of whom Grant had been at Oxford with. They included Nigella Lawson, daughter of the former Chancellor of the Exchequer Nigel Lawson, and her journalist brother Dominic. Nigella, who went on to become a food writer and achieve fame as the 'Domestic Goddess', had been a leading light of the Oxford party scene – a role she continued in London. 'Hugh was in with a very arty set,' says Debra. 'They modelled themselves on the decadent set of the 1930s and they used to wear fancy dress and go to masked balls. It was quite a big group and it was completely different to the set Liz had been involved with before.' At last Elizabeth was part of a lifestyle that she had always yearned to join. Hugh would take her to his undergraduate reunion dinners and the way that she looked and spoke was now backed up by a glamorous, bohemian way of life.

And far from being looked down on by Hugh's university chums, Elizabeth immediately inspired their respect. 'She was so obviously incredibly street-smart,' one friend was quoted as saying. 'Very cool and observant. If there was any intimidating going on, it was coming from Elizabeth. She never came across as an intellectual, but she was as sharp as a tack.' But Elizabeth's natural compulsion to show off caused her to come a cropper one night when she was partying with her new friends in a London bar. She was dancing on a table when she ignominiously fell off, breaking her elbow.

Her pride still wounded from being dumped by Thomas Arklie, she could not resist letting him know that she was no longer pining for him. 'A month after we split she sent me a rather blunt letter telling me she had just finished a film and had fallen in love with Hugh Grant,' he recalls. The couple did not remain friends and when Arklie bumped into Liz and Hugh at a restaurant in Notting Hill not long afterwards he did not stop and chat. 'It was kind of awkward,' he admits. 'I kept a distance because I don't think it's wise for an ex-boyfriend to hang around. She and Hugh probably have more in common in terms of background. He is very well educated and that probably suits Liz.'

Although they had been together for four years and planned to marry, all Elizabeth has said about Arklie is, 'He was very sweet but we were completely different.' After their split he dated the singer Sinitta for several years. He now lives in Los

Angeles where he works in a nightclub and is trying to make it as an actor. He says that he will always have a fond place in his heart for Liz because 'she was the first girl I ever fell hopelessly in love with'. But despite Hollywood being a small world and Liz being a film producer, he has no contact with her.

Debra Holder knew that her friend had been more hurt by losing Arklie than she cared to admit. But she could see that Liz seemed a lot happier with Hugh Grant than she had been with his strong-willed predecessor. 'Liz wrote to me when she started seeing Hugh and she seemed more settled then,' she said. 'I thought Hugh was a bit wimpy. I don't think he was the type of bloke that she felt afraid to lose. With Tommy it was always a challenge because she felt that she might lose him. And she was attracted by that. I think she craves a bit of excitement. She wants someone who can keep her on her toes sexually in the relationship. But with Hugh it was easier for her and she seemed happier.'

Debra also got the impression that Liz was just as smitten with Hugh's friends as she was with him. 'She now had stability because Hugh had a lot of friends in the world of film and arts,' she explains. 'Being with him could open doors for her but I don't think she was premeditated about it. I think they really did get on well. They hit it off and felt comfortable with each other. She was like a sister to him in a way.'

Rowing in the Wind was Elizabeth's second film role. She had made her screen debut at the age of 21, appearing in a scene from *Aria*. The movie, released in 1988 and produced by Don Boyd, featured ten leading filmmakers' interpretations of classic arias. Elizabeth was directed in her role by Bruce Beresford and was required to do little except take her clothes off and mime topless. She had no qualms about undressing for the cameras and her appearance *sans* top probably went some way to distract from her attempts at miming.

But her big break was being cast as the heroine in *Christabel*, Dennis Potter's BBC adaptation of Christabel Bielenberg's life story. Having bared her breasts in her first two roles, this was a part for which Elizabeth would be required to keep her top on, but she did not allow this to put her off. Neither was she deterred by the fact that half the actresses in Britain appeared to be after the role, every one of them more experienced than she was. At the audition, she was told by the producer Kenith Trodd that it was a part 'every actress in London is killing for at the moment'. Actresses in the frame to play Christabel included Imogen Stubbs, who had recently starred in the BBC's acclaimed adaptation of D. H. Lawrence's *The Rainbow*, and Phoebe Nicholls, one of the stars of ITV's celebrated series *Brideshead Revisited*.

Elizabeth, on the other hand, was almost completely unknown as an actress. *Rowing in the Wind* had not yet been released and her only claim to fame had been a fleeting appearance in a television commercial for Schweppes. But this was actually to work in her favour because, as she had nothing on tape to show the producers, they had no option but to give her a screen test. 'I didn't do any preparation for *Christabel* because I didn't think I'd get it,' she later admitted. 'I thought they were only offering me the screen test in order to go through the motions of appearing to be fair.'

But as soon as he heard her speak, Kenith Trodd knew that she would be perfect for the role. Christabel Bielenberg had a distinctive upper-class clipped tone, almost identical to that which Elizabeth had been adopting for years. And just as Elizabeth's beauty had made gibbering wrecks of Derek Nimmo and Leslie Phillips, so too did it now work its magic on Kenith Trodd. 'There was something throwback about Elizabeth,' Trodd mused. 'It was like 50 years that hadn't been. She was so luminous. You could not watch her on film and think about anything else. It was not just a question of bone structure or of the camera loving her. There was something else – a way of being.'

And when Dennis Potter sat down to watch the screen tests he was similarly affected. 'Who,' he asked with wonder, 'is she?' Despite her lack of a track record, the playwright was sufficiently captivated to pick Elizabeth to be his Christabel – and also to take her out to lunch. He and Trodd were not the only ones to be bowled over by Elizabeth's beauty and presence. Actor Hugh Simon, who was one of her co-stars, well remembers the moment he first laid eyes on her. 'I went to the read through, which was at north Acton, and I was quite nervous because it was my first television role,' he explained. 'I walked into the room, which was crowded with people, and in the centre of the room was this absolutely beautiful, stunning girl in jeans and a sweater. She didn't have on any make-up or anything like that, but she was just absolutely knockout gorgeous. And my chin hit the floor. I picked my chin back up and said to myself, "I don't know who you are but I think you're playing Christabel." She could have been in the business for years and years. From the confidence that she gave off you wouldn't have known that it was her first big role.'

Virtually every chap who came into contact with Elizabeth was mesmerized by her beauty. 'The first thing to be said about Elizabeth Hurley is that men may be unreliable witnesses about her,' observed journalist Elizabeth Grice, writing in *The Sunday Times* in 1989. Liz, she said, clearly had a talent to bemuse the male of the species and *The Sunday Times*'s photographer, Bob Collier, had apparently needed no less than three sessions at Liz's South Kensington flat in order to perfect his portrait of her. When Grice asked Collier how he had found his subject, his solemn reply was, 'Very desirable.'

Potter's adaptation was scheduled to go out on BBC2 in four parts in November, 1988. It was the corporation's biggest project of the year and as its star, three-and-a-half million pounds of licence-payers' money was resting on Elizabeth's young shoulders. This was a fact of which she was only too aware and also in her mind was the knowledge that appearing in such a high-profile drama might open doors for her in America. At that time British actress Joanne Whalley, who had starred in Dennis Potter's previous BBC hit *The Singing Detective*, had managed to carve out a successful Hollywood career on the back of its success. Everyone was watching to see if Potter would do for Elizabeth Hurley what he had done for Joanne Whalley.

The story was based on Yorkshire-born Christabel Burton, a niece of the newspaper barons Lords Rothermere and Northcliffe, who married a young German lawyer called Peter Bielenberg in 1934. The following year she went to live with him in Germany, but when war was declared she found herself cut off from her family, married to 'the enemy' and, because she had been forced to take up German citizenship on marriage, an 'enemy' herself. The Bielenbergs refused to leave Germany and Peter Bielenberg instead plotted to oust Hitler. But after the failed July 1944 attempt on the Führer's life, he was imprisoned in the notorious Ravensbruck concentration camp.

Christabel was granted a visit and Peter managed to smuggle her his version of events on lavatory paper, which he had hidden inside a matchbox. She learned it by heart and bravely volunteered herself for interrogation by the Nazis. After nine gruelling hours she had managed to convince the Gestapo of her husband's innocence. Peter Bielenberg was released from the concentration camp and sent to a punishment squad, from which he later escaped to the Black Forest.

Christabel's subsequent autobiography, *The Past is Myself*, was a bestseller and when Dennis Potter read it he fell in love with the story, describing it as 'a total celebration of married love'. The couple made their home in Ireland after the war and invited Liz to visit them there. 'Elizabeth is a very nice girl indeed,' said Mrs Bielenberg afterwards. 'And of course if this works it will be the chance of a lifetime for her.' For her part, Elizabeth was full of awe for the old lady. 'She must have been incredibly brave,' she said. 'It would have been so easy for both of them just to go along with the Nazis. But they wouldn't. I was terrified by just reading the scene in the script when she meets her husband in Ravensbruck. That was frightening enough. But when I met them both in Ireland I knew how to play it. I didn't need to ask.

'We got on immediately and as soon as I saw them sitting at their kitchen table having a sandwich the whole thing fell into place. When you see what ordinary lovely people they are it stops you being too actressy or over-dramatic. Christabel is a sweet and lovely person. Although she is nearly 80 she still acts as though she's about twenty. I felt a great responsibility towards her when we filmed the series. She told me not to cry in any of the scenes. She said, "Promise me you won't make her a drip." But we never talked about her courage, only about what she wore in Germany during the war and whether she had a perm and if she used make-up.'

Having met the couple, Elizabeth agreed wholeheartedly with Potter's description of the story being a celebration of married love. 'Some people might laugh and think that is naff,' she said. 'I don't. This is an enormous story of love and fidelity – and what could be better than that? Christabel came from the upper-class landed gentry in England but Dennis Potter also shows their strength and integrity. They were not fickle, bright young things.'

Elizabeth and the playwright appeared to have formed something of a mutual admiration society. He described her as 'self-possessed' and had been sufficiently impressed to hire her over the heads of far more experienced actresses. She for her part was in awe of the dramatist's intellect. 'He is a lovely person and so clever,' she praised. 'I love clever people. Some just radiate it and he is one of them.' Working with the legendary writer was also to leave her with a love of old songs. 'My favourite is "Something Stupid" by Frank and Nancy Sinatra and all those classic 1930s and 1940s songs that Dennis Potter uses in his plays,' she said in a subsequent interview.

For the role Elizabeth had to have her waist-length hair cut into a jaw-length bob and dyed brown. But a legacy of her punk years was to cause problems for the make-up department. Elizabeth's nose ring had left a scar, which she still has to this day, and the hole had to be carefully disguised with make-up. She spent six months of 1988 filming in Budapest, Dundee and London. As she was in virtually every scene she ended up bonding more with the production crew than with her fellow actors. 'While others came and went I got on brilliantly with the crew because I was with them all the time,' she explained. 'Being stuck in Budapest, there was nothing to do but go out for a beer or two with the boys.' While she was in Hungary Elizabeth was given a mink coat to keep out the bitter cold. But back home in London it caused something of a stink when she chose to wear it in Camden. She was chased down the street by people who objected to her wearing dead animals. 'But I do enjoy wearing it,' she admitted.

Elizabeth was delighted to have secured the role of Christabel. 'I realize that Potter is taking an enormous gamble in casting me for the part,' she acknowledged. 'It's an absolutely super part. There's some quite good love scenes in it. No bonking, but some good honest snogging. I am very lucky this has happened at twenty-two. At 28 I would be frightened it might stop then, but failure never really occurs to me now. Some friends who are actors tend to be rather down about their chances. I have never been down and being with down people depresses me. Maybe the security I had as a child helps me there. I wouldn't have started acting if I didn't think I'd succeed.' With the arrogance of youth she even attempted indifference. 'I could always go and do something else if acting did not work out,' she reasoned. 'I am still young – and irresponsible.'

But the reality was somewhat different. Elizabeth was extremely nervous of being on a film set and initially sought refuge in her trailer. 'I hid in my caravan for four days until I had to go in front of the cameras for a couple of minutes,' she subsequently admitted. 'I was absolutely terrified of even getting a cup of tea.' She found comfort by reading Enid Blyton and old pony books from her childhood. During breaks in filming she could often be seen crouched over her knitting or working away at a piece of tapestry to settle her nerves.

When the programme was shown to the press, Elizabeth disappeared just as the lights were about to go down, saying that she was going in search of a sausage roll and a drink. She was understandably worried about what the critics' reaction would be to her first major role, but she needn't have worried. 'The scene where she listened to the confession of a SS concentration camp killer, who spoke like a devil sick of sin, was one of the most memorable in Potter's canon, no small compliment,' wrote the *Observer*'s television reviewer. Elizabeth's performance was also praised at the 1988 Cannes Television Festival. No less flattering was Peter Bielenberg's reaction to her portrayal of his wife. He and Christabel burst into tears at the memories it brought back. 'Elizabeth is very convincing,' he said. 'I shed a tear once or twice when I watched her.'

The Times' film critic Sean Macaulay believes that Liz's performance in *Christabel* was possibly the finest of her career to date. '*Christabel* was the drama in which she showed the most ability and promise,' he says. 'She has described herself as being a melancholy and serious actress, which is strange when you consider the other work she's done in *Austin Powers* and *EDtv*. But she seems to think that's her natural mode and oddly enough *Christabel* seems to suggest that it is.'

By 1988, Elizabeth and Hugh were living together at his flat in Earls Court, West London. She also had her own flat in Fulham, bought at the beginning of the year as an investment, but she let this to her brother Michael, by then a 19-year-old student at King's College. From the very start of their relationship, she and Hugh had to get used to the fact that they would inevitably spend a lot of time apart. While she was making *Christabel*, Hugh Grant had been filming a series called *Champagne Charlie* in France. He then flew to America to begin work on a project called *Dangerous Love*, for America's CBS network. Although *Four Weddings and A Funeral* was still some way in the future, Grant had already made something of a name for himself as an actor and had been voted Best Actor at the 1987 Venice Film Festival for his role in *Maurice*.

During a period of what actors euphemistically refer to as resting, Elizabeth busied herself by organizing the complete redecoration of Hugh's apartment. She was also a keen gardener and set about transforming their roof terrace into a miniature English garden. 'We have honeysuckle, clematis, old roses, lilies and lots of sweet peas,' she said proudly. In early interviews she shared this and other little snippets of their life together, describing everything from what they liked to eat to the clothes they liked to wear. She was not a keen cook, she disclosed, because she 'loathed' the inevitable washing up. Moreover, she believed that men should do the cooking. 'I am only going to marry someone if he's a good cook,' she announced.

Hugh may have been a pretty boy, but Elizabeth wasn't about to let him into the bathroom first. 'I can't bear boys done up in designer kit, fighting for my mirror,' she said bluntly. 'I like boys who look like stockbrokers in dark Savile Row suits. Hugh looks good in Ralph Lauren, which is every American's idea of what Englishmen wear. When he puts on his suits he looks so sweet.' Elizabeth took a wifely interest in Hugh's clothes, but was not quite as hands on with his wardrobe as he was with hers. Revealing how he would lay her clothes out on the bed for her before an evening out, she told how he also bought most of her clothes. 'He always goes shopping for me,' she said. 'We have the same taste. He likes me in hotpants and hates me in big baggy things. He bought me a wonderful Chanel black wool jacket which I wear as a little tunic dress. I like to look sexy. I like anything naughty and I adore sexy lingerie. Hugh always buys me sexy knickers in Paris or New York. He says English knickers just aren't as nice.'

As they began to attract press attention as a 'celebrity couple', the pair's pretentious mannerisms soon draw comment. 'They both use an aristo-slang of "beastlies" and "frightfuls" and have developed mannerisms that are positively regal,' the *Observer*'s Andrew Anthony noted. 'Grant is in the habit of fluttering his eyelashes and toying with his jacket pockets like Prince Charles on a shy day, while Hurley becomes a queen in front of a flashgun.' Elizabeth loved the fact that she and Hugh were so similar. Their backgrounds were virtual mirror images: both had fathers who had been in the army and schoolteachers for mothers, and both were second children who knew what it was like to grow up in the shadow of older, more glamorous siblings. They even looked alike and were often taken for sister and brother, something which amused them a great deal. However, Hugh did not share Elizabeth's total inability to be tidy. 'He is the opposite,' she said. 'He is obsessive about everything being in its place.'

Elizabeth accompanied Hugh on his promotional tours when she could, although she professed to dislike being seen as simply an appendage on his arm. But when the BBC sold *Christabel* around the world she was asked to go to the States to help promote the show there. It was an opportunity she jumped at. 'Some people just won't do promotions at all,' she said. 'I think it's awfully bad manners to turn it down. It is part and parcel of the job. If someone takes a chance and gives you a wonderful opportunity, it's the least you can do.' She travelled out to Los Angeles in January 1989, accompanied by Hugh. This gave Elizabeth the chance to turn the tables. 'Neither of us likes the bimbo role very much, but it's his turn now,' she said firmly.

As an actress, Elizabeth knew the way she looked was extremely important. And after being on a film set for six months making *Christabel* she felt that she needed to lose weight. 'I was on set from 6 a.m. to 9 p.m. every day and living on location catering which is very stodgy,' she said. Despite her hatred of exercise, she bit the bullet and joined a gym. 'It's full of Sloaney women who don't work,' she complained. 'Exercise is misery. I do aerobics every day and swimming but I've lost half a stone.' She also took up horse-riding and toyed with the idea of learning to play polo. But while other women envied her good looks, Elizabeth considered herself to be far from perfect. She admitted she was 'feverishly jealous' of Jamie Lee Curtis's body. 'I adore her legs and things,' she said. 'Also Elizabeth Taylor when she was young.'

Despite the success of *Christabel*, Elizabeth made it clear that she wasn't only in the market for serious roles. 'There aren't many Dennis Potters around,' she acknowledged. 'So if Kenny Everett asks me to guest on one of his shows I'll be happy to oblige!' But she turned down roles in two foreign films in 1989, choosing instead to play the lead role in the television mini-series *Act of Will*. The story, about a woman who becomes a leading fashion designer, was based on Barbara Taylor Bradford's best-selling novel. Unfortunately for Liz, it was voted a stinker. 'Her performance in *Act of Will* was so forced it was like sausage meat,' said film critic Karen Krizanovich.

After *Act of Will*, Liz was hired for a German-made film called *The Skipper*. The movie starred Jurgen Prochnow as the sailor with a tragic past and Liz and 22-year-old Patsy Kensit as the hairdressers from Leeds whom he befriends. The skipper takes the girls on a trip to Barbados in his prized yacht, but the voyage turns to horror in the middle of the Atlantic. Off-screen events were hardly plain sailing either. The film was shot in Malta where the temperature was 115 degrees in the shade and being on top of each other for long periods led to frayed tempers. The yacht on which the film was set was built to hold four people but the cast and crew numbered more than forty.

'Filming was very hard,' said Patsy Kensit. 'We were at close quarters twelve hours a day and it naturally led to tensions. But the worst thing was the crew couldn't accept that Elizabeth and I might want to do something other than filming. Malta is a lovely place for a holiday but after three months you're clawing your way out.' Kensit, with whom Liz struck up a friendship, explained that problems also arose because of the different methods of filming. 'In Europe the actors have to obey all the producer's wishes,' she said. 'With *The Skipper* there were many disagreements on set. We often felt no one appreciated us. I'm the type that has to argue and fiddle with a scene until it's right.'

Matters were not helped by the fact that Liz and Patsy declared virtual war on the German crew and cast. Elizabeth had major bust-ups with Jurgen Prochnow, star of the award-winning German U-boat drama *Das Boot*. 'He was horrible – the vile Jurgen,' she said afterwards. 'I can't believe anyone would employ him. He's so repellent.' But Liz's and Patsy's ball-breaking attitude did not go down too well with the director Peter Keglevic. 'Something so strange happened,' he said. 'I don't understand young women any more. Crudely put, today's men must be more and more afraid that today's young women will kick them where it hurts.'

Despite the *News of the World*'s confident assertion that the film had 'everything it needs to be a box-office success', it wasn't. And Karen Krizanovich was not impressed by Liz's performance. 'Apalling,' she said. 'It was like a car accident – so bad you had to watch it.' Liz's friendship with Patsy Kensit looked like ending up as the girlie equivalent of a holiday romance. 'We were brilliant friends while filming but had nothing in common really apart from the fact that we could laugh about the make-up lady's fat legs,' Liz later told journalist Garth Pearce.

The Skipper was not the only foreign film in which Elizabeth was to fall out with the people she was working with. While making the Frederick Forsyth thriller *Death Has a Bad Reputation* in Italy in 1990 she had a clash of wills with the producers. Liz had been cast as Julia Latham, a hard-nosed television reporter on the trail of the terrorist Carlos the Jackal. But as the fight against evil unfolded in the back streets of Rome, the real battle was over the length of Liz's skirt. She saw her character as a tough Kate Adie-like figure but the film's producers wanted a glamour puss. 'Julia is a go-getter, she has a hard edge but the Italians wanted a girl running around in strappy sandals and designer shorts,' moaned Liz, seemingly oblivious to the fact that was why she had probably been hired for the role in the first place.

'I kept saying no because if you are trying to play somebody real you should be in your jeans and T-shirt.' But it was an argument she was never going to win. The programme-makers had wanted a gorgeous leggy girl to play the part and, having hired one, they weren't prepared to see her covered up. 'We had terrible rows and I ended up too glam in a minidress,' said Liz. 'I wanted my 501s but they got me into a suede shirt.'

Liz also spent three months of 1990 making a film for Channel 4 on the idyllic Caribbean island of Dominica. *The Orchid House*, a four-part adaptation of Phyllis Shand Allfrey's novel about the island, starred Elizabeth as a rich young widow. It was the first time that an international film had been shot on the island and filming did not exactly go smoothly. The main problem was the weather. The island has up to four hours' rain a day so the crew had to plan filming around the showers. And when the rain was heavy the roads became impassable until the water drained away. There was no main airport on the island, just a basic landing strip, and there were not enough hotels to accommodate the cast and crew. Islanders offered spare bedrooms and also appeared as extras in the film, but things were thrown into chaos when the Dominican Prime Minister decided to call a general election. 'It was hilarious because filming came to a complete standstill as all the islanders went off to vote and to party,' said Liz.

But despite the problems of filming in the Caribbean, Liz found it a wonderful place to be. 'I was totally bowled over by Dominica,' she said. 'You could say that I fell in love with the island. It is stunningly beautiful.' She also got on 'unexpectedly well' with her co-star Frances Barber. 'Both of us thought it would be hate on sight,' Liz admitted. 'She's "right on" – wears black plimsolls, lives in Camden and reads *The Guardian* – whereas I am completely the opposite. But we became good friends.' Such good friends, in fact, that after just a few weeks on the island the pair moved out of their small hotel and into a beautiful house in the hills. 'It was such a pretty house,' Liz enthused. 'It was under a mango tree and the whole ambience was so relaxing.'

Best of all for an untidy person like Liz, the house came equipped with no fewer than four local housekeepers to wait on her hand and foot. 'One of the best things about the place were the house boys who were there to look after us,' she said. 'They were wonderful and they really spoiled us. They cooked for us, cleaned the place and even picked up our knickers from the floor. After we'd finished filming we would stroll home and the boys would be waiting there with glorious reggae music roaring out of a ghetto blaster. The whole island had a carnival atmosphere.' Apart from the difficulties of trying to get anything done in such a laid-back place, the only other downside was the food. 'Chicken and rice, the staple diet of the Dominicans, is all very nice for a few days, but after a while it gets rather boring,' Liz admitted. 'I found myself dreaming about wandering around a Marks and Spencer food hall and buying lots of delicious things. One can only eat so much chicken, rice and mangoes!'

By the end of 1990, Liz was also dreaming of trying her luck in America. Starring in major British television series was all well and good, but she had been there and done that. She was keen to move on to bigger and better things, and Hollywood beckoned …

4 The Viles

The week Elizabeth spent in Hollywood promoting *Christabel* had given her a taste for life in the glamorous film capital. Being naturally impatient, she felt frustrated by the limited amount of work open to her in Britain. America offered the kind of opportunities that simply didn't exist at home and she realized that if she was ever going to make the big time she needed to be in Los Angeles. Whereas in England she had to sit around and wait for the phone to ring, in Hollywood there were movie deals being done every minute of the day. There was also the lucrative US television market to break into, where those who succeeded in making it big could earn more money than many movie stars. Elizabeth wanted a slice of the action and by the end of 1990 she was finalizing plans to move there full-time.

Some people considered that she should stay in Britain and build on the success she had achieved in *Christabel*, but Liz was having none of it. Thinking it best to take her chances before she was 'too old, married or child-bound', in January 1991 she packed up her Evelyn Waugh books and sexy French underwear and moved to LA. Strangely, given that she was in a live-in relationship with Hugh Grant, she was to make the move alone. Hugh was said to be too busy filming his role as Chopin in the movie *Impromptu* to go with her, but in truth he did not want to go. Although he was already enjoying limited success in America, he had no desire to live there and steadfastly refused to leave London. Having to leave one's boyfriend behind in another country may have deterred some people from making the move, but not Elizabeth. Her ambition was such that nothing was going to stop her trying her damnedest to make it big in America.

When journalists expressed surprise that she was going without him, her reply appeared to be almost dismissive of their relationship. 'We haven't any marriage plans,' she said bluntly. 'He's 30, which is more the marrying age, but it's not right for me to think about settling down yet. Even now I don't feel I have a lot of independence because we do virtually everything together and I am an uncaged bird.' And in an interview later the same year she implied that the romance might not last for much longer. 'We have had our ups and downs,' she told journalist Garth Pearce. 'I maintain that I would not be interested in settling down and having children with an actor. We would be apart too much. Life is difficult because you are constantly jealous when the other person is away – he may be having more fun than you are. Even worse is when you are both not working, waiting for the phone to ring with offers. But after four years together Hugh is still my best friend and I cannot imagine life without him.'

However, the British actress Charlotte Lewis, who became a close friend of Elizabeth's when she arrived in Los Angeles, claims that she actively wanted to be apart from Hugh at that time. 'She told me that she was feeling a little possessed by the whole thing and had to get away so she could have some kind of space between them and focus on her own thing,' she said.

Liz appeared confident about her chances of achieving success Stateside and even at that early stage in her career expressed a desire to get into film production. 'It's an enormous gamble because there are things I could do here even if they are parts I'm not that fascinated by,' she said. 'But to be there is so exciting. You're suddenly off to meet Warren Beatty for a film role and there are such big things happening. I sit around in England and get offered an episode in *Inspector Morse*. No disrespect, I've done one and enjoyed it but …'

Elizabeth had indeed been invited to meet Warren Beatty. Having been shown some film of her by a casting agent, the star sent his limousine to collect her for breakfast at his £3 million mansion overlooking Beverly Hills. 'When an invitation like that comes along you don't refuse, even if you think it might get a little awkward,' said Elizabeth. 'Everyone told me no one turns Warren Beatty down when he asks them round.' It was obviously on her mind that the legendary Lothario might be planning to introduce her to the Hollywood casting couch, and she seemed almost disappointed when Beatty's interest in her turned out to be purely professional. 'I was driven to this amazing house where we had some breakfast, which he prepared himself, and he was a real gentleman,' she told *The Sun*. 'After looking me up and down for half an hour he said, "Baby, you're just too young." I took it that he was referring to the part he was considering me for, not for anything else. In any case his mother was there so I don't suppose he could try anything.'

It wasn't the first time that Elizabeth was to miss out on a part because of her almost adolescent looks. The Americans considered that she didn't look at all like someone in her twenties and this often went against her at auditions. 'I never dress up so I am regarded as a bit of an oddity in LA where they tend to cast me as 17-year-old ingénues,' complained Liz, who was by then aged twenty-six. 'I was quite insulted when I went for an audition and was told I didn't look mature enough to play a twenty-two-year-old.'

She also appeared to be displeased that no one had requested sexual favours from her in return for work. 'So far no one has ever tried to get me to go to bed with them to get a role or ask me to show my boobs, although I know it happens,' she said. 'I've never had an improper proposition career-wise. I wish I had in some ways, it might be interesting. I'm sure it goes on and it's not always the poor little girl being duped. Some people make a decent career out of it.' Liz consoled herself by telling herself that she probably looked too confident to be taken advantage of. 'I must look as if I'd give a great big right hook back,' she concluded. 'Of course I can because I do kick-boxing. Maybe it shows in my face, I don't know.'

In interviews she revealed a readiness to strip for the cameras – providing, of course, that the role absolutely demanded it. 'I don't mind the idea of taking my clothes off,' she said. 'It's not a big thing. I don't like the idea of prancing around naked just for the sake of it, that's not my cup of tea. But if it's all part of the plot, then why not? You don't turn down a part because of a love scene. On the other hand I don't believe that I have to take off my clothes and do a *Playboy* spread to succeed.'

But when she flew back to Britain in March 1991 to promote *The Orchid House*, she was clearly already having doubts about her career move. On the one hand she obviously enjoyed the kudos that being based in Hollywood gave her with the British Press, but she also gave the distinct impression that she would give her eye teeth to be working in Britain. 'I really love LA and have a wonderful apartment with a swimming pool and Jacuzzi on the roof,' she boasted. 'I've been pretty busy, but when I've had a quiet afternoon it's glorious to read a good book by the pool, or just take in the amazing view.' But she admitted she would prefer to work in Britain again, and went on to advertise herself available for work. 'I suppose like most people I went there for the work and I shouldn't complain because I have a good life in LA,' she said. 'But I've never made a film in England, it's always been in Europe or America. So if anyone out there is still making films in England, give me a call.'

In truth, Liz had discovered that it was more difficult to get work in America than she had envisaged. Finding herself to be just one of many pretty faces in Hollywood, a small fish in a very big pond, she sought refuge in all things English. She fell in with a group of feckless, upper-crust Brits who included the aristocratic Henry Dent-Brocklehurst, heir to Sudeley Castle in Gloucestershire. Liz had met the former heroin addict soon after her arrival in LA and the pair formed a close friendship. Brocklehurst even lived with her at her flat for two months, although they have always denied rumours of a romance. Others in the set were journalist William Cash, the eccentric son of Tory MP Bill Cash, and public schoolboy-turned restaurateur William Annesley. Liz and her new pals looked down their collective nose at the native inhabitants of La La land and dubbed themselves the Viles, in honour of the Evelyn Waugh book. Elizabeth was one of the only female members of the Viles, a situation that suited her enormously because it ensured that she got maximum attention. According to her former friend Toby Young, Liz occupied the role of 'den mother' within the group. 'She wanted every man in the room's attention,' he has said. 'She was an egalitarian exhibitionist.'

Not long after she arrived in America, Elizabeth gave up her small apartment and went to live with the British film producer Julia Verdin. They were introduced by Hugh Grant, who used to live opposite Verdin in London. Julia's LA house was located just off Sunset Boulevard in trendy West Hollywood. It had been built in the 1920s and had five bedrooms, all of which were usually filled with visiting friends. In 1992 a third girl came to live at the house: wealthy banker's daughter Birgit Cunningham. An outgoing, 29-year-old society blonde, Cunningham had become bored with the London party scene and arrived in Los Angeles determined to live life to the full. She had been educated at Roedean, the famous girls' school near Brighton, before landing a job selling yachts to the super-rich. Upon arrival in LA, she got a job working as an executive secretary in a Hollywood studio and subsequently had an affair with actor Kevin Costner.

Julia Verdin was also a party animal and her home was well known as one of *the* places to be in Hollywood. 'We used to have parties two or three times a week and lots of big stars came,' says Birgit. 'People like Jack Nicholson. I remember once when Julian Lennon was having a party at his place up in the Hollywood hills and the word went round about a party "at Jules's" place.

But about 30 people got the wrong end of the stick and ended up at Julia's house instead. Julian Lennon was pretty miffed! Some people thought it was a really wild house but we'd sit and have a couple of vodka tonics and that was about it. There was a nice atmosphere but it wasn't wild.'

Although she and Elizabeth were not destined to become close friends, Birgit nonetheless enjoyed being in her company. 'When Liz walked into a room you felt you were in the centre in the world because she was there,' she says. 'She had loads of energy, and a great sense of humour. I was really in awe of her.' But she also reveals that despite her subsequent image as a jet-setter, Liz was not a wild person. 'She is incredibly domesticated,' she says. 'She was always gardening and the garden looked fantastic when she lived there. She would be busy reupholstering furniture or decorating, and we had a piano in the house which she was learning to play. She was quite good too, she's definitely not your average Hollywood actress.' Neither was Elizabeth particularly glamorous in those early days. 'She would wear jeans, albeit quite tight ones, and big jumpers,' says Birgit. 'I remember her making sausage and mash in the kitchen wearing no make-up and with her hair tied back.'

Elizabeth was often away visiting Hugh in London but Birgit always knew when her flatmate was at home. 'We had wooden floors and Liz used to walk everywhere very fast in her high-heeled shoes,' she says. Liz also had a slavering male following her everywhere – her pet Alsatian Nico, whom she had rescued and was totally devoted to. 'He was a bit of a psycho dog because he'd been stabbed by burglars before Liz rescued him,' explains Birgit. 'As a result he thought that everyone was a burglar.'

Although Liz and Birgit were sharing a house, they were moving in very different circles socially. While Birgit enthusiastically threw herself into the Hollywood party scene, drugs and all, Liz remained loftily aloof. 'She never seemed that interested in the parties, she wasn't even at the house a lot of the time,' says Birgit. 'She was more interested in her upper-class English friends. There was a definite them and us thing going on. The whole drug thing was taking place amongst the more debauched Hollywood set but I think the English *Vile Bodies* crowd considered themselves far above that. I never saw Liz take drugs and I have a feeling that she is actually really against them. I remember her looking down on people who did drugs. She would dismiss them as incompetent imbeciles. It wasn't her thing at all. I had gone out to LA an innocent but within six months I had changed. You would be offered drugs several times a day and when I came back to London in 1997 I had to go into rehab. But Liz likes to be in control.'

However, the Americans in Hollywood worked extremely hard, getting into the office at seven in the morning and often not leaving until eleven at night. In stark contrast, the Viles, when they worked at all, were incredibly laid back. 'British people in LA in the 1990's were pretty louche,' explains Sean Macaulay. 'There was a fairly decadent, lazy, moneyed upper class contingent who would play cricket and sunbathe. They just treated LA a bit like a holiday resort.' At that stage in her life, Elizabeth was happy to go along with that and she and her friends strove to emulate the bright young things of the Roaring Twenties. 'I noticed that she started to behave like a character from *Vile Bodies*,' says Birgit. 'She would quote the characters chapter and verse. It's one thing to be influenced by a book, it's quite another to really live it and she absolutely lived it.

'She was so British. I would be going to all the Hollywood premières but Liz would rather go to the pub or watch the cricket. We didn't have a lot in common. I was going on Lear jets and yachts while she was staying in drafty English country houses. Her friends didn't have money, most of them were penniless, but they would sit about drinking very nice wine and having big Britishy dinners. I was invited to some of their dos and it was just like being in a civilized country house in England. It was really weird – very, very surreal. It would really annoy me because we would be sitting in a pub on a Saturday or Sunday, with the sun blaring outside, drinking a pint. I hated it, absolutely hated it. It was the same with the Sunday lunches. We'd be sitting indoors, having a sit-down formal Sunday lunch while it was sunny outside, eating such heavy food that you couldn't do anything afterwards.'

But there was generally a conspicuous absentee from the Viles' get-togethers: Hugh Grant. The fact that his girlfriend lived there had done nothing to abate his dislike of Los Angeles, and it was a major hurdle for the couple. 'Hugh doesn't like LA at all and I think that is going to be a problem,' Liz told *The Sun* in an interview. Such was his loathing of the city that he would seldom deign to visit her there. 'I didn't meet Hugh until much, much later because he didn't come round to the house,' says Birgit. 'He couldn't cope with the way the house was. There were always people staying there and coming and going. You'd arrive home to find several people in the living room and you might not know any of them.'

But for Elizabeth, there was nowhere better to be. 'I love the palm trees and the massive billboards,' she enthused, a year after moving to LA. 'It still excites me, even though the place has no culture and is really pretty sick.' And she appeared pragmatic about her separation from Grant. 'Of course I miss Hugh, but I've got my work and I know he's at the other end of a telephone line if I need a shoulder to cry on,' she said matter-of-factly. 'Six weeks is about the longest we allow to be apart, but generally we manage to see quite a lot of each other.'

Their long-distance relationship may have appeared odd to many people but it was not totally unheard of for couples in their profession to live in separate countries. 'With actors it is quite usual for them to be on the other side of the world to each other,' says Birgit. 'I would say that they had a really nice relationship. Hugh would send her lots of very affectionate faxes. In fact, I started despising him because the fax machine was in my bedroom and all these long faxes would spill out at three or four o clock in the morning and continue for about an hour. I didn't read them – I couldn't have even if I'd wanted to because of his scrawly writing – but I wasn't interested in reading things in the middle of the night.

'It used to annoy me a bit and I vowed to have it out with him when I saw him. But of course when I met him he was so charming that I forgave him instantly. We met at the Cannes Film Festival and he was really famous by then, as was Liz. But he came up to me and shook my hand and said, "Oh, Birgit, I've heard so much about you," which was really weird coming from someone that famous.'

In 1991 Elizabeth had starred in *The Young Indiana Jones Chronicles*, an American show that was due to be screened on British TV the following January. More importantly, her name was in the frame to play Lady Chatterley in the much-trumpeted BBC version of D. H. Lawrence's book. The major £4 million series, adapted by controversial director Ken Russell, promised to be a 'no-holds-barred account' of the love affair between Lady Connie Chatterley and her gamekeeper. Russell, who had previously filmed another sexually explicit Lawrence classic, *Women in Love*, stated that he would not allow his work to be censored, and said the series would retain every explicit scene. It was due to begin filming in May 1992 and the smart money was on Elizabeth for the lead role. For, like Nimmo, Phillips and Potter before him, Russell had fallen under the Hurley spell. He called her 'the most beautiful young woman I have ever seen and with incredible talent' and there was little doubt in anyone's mind that she would play her sexy ladyship.

'I read Lady Chatterley at school and thought it was terrific,' she said, obviously believing that she had the role sewn up. 'I will be going in to it with my eyes well and truly open. As for possible nude scenes, it's not like posing for *Playboy*, is it? If certain things are within the context of the story then I have to take it seriously.' Elizabeth badly needed the high-profile role back in Britain for she was still finding it difficult to crack Hollywood. 'It's incredibly hard for people to break in,' she acknowledged in an interview with the *Mail on Sunday*. 'But it's quite an attractive lifestyle and I tell myself I'll stay until I'm thirty.'

Chapter 4

Having been faced with two years of near constant rejection from the major Hollywood studios, her luck changed in 1992 when she landed a part in the Warner Brothers action thriller *Passenger 57*. The movie, about a hijacking on board an aeroplane, starred Wesley Snipes as the hero and featured Liz as a gun-toting terrorist posing as an air hostess. Although her part was a small one – her character was dead before cinemagoers were halfway through their popcorn – the film was a box-office hit and shot straight to the top of the US film charts in its first week. It was a significant break for Liz. 'Being in a film that has taken a bit of money helps open a few extra doors,' she acknowledged.

Preparing for the role also triggered an interest in shooting and, surprisingly for someone who had made their boyfriend leave the armed forces, she became a member of the exclusive Beverly Hills Gun Club. 'I shoot 9 mm,' she said. 'I like it, it's fun. I don't like to boast but I'm really good and I'm hooked on it. I'm doing a course and they tell you all about the bullets that do the most damage. It can be pretty scary, especially when you see all the weirdoes on the range with guns strapped to them, shooting like they are Dirty Harry. I haven't bought a gun but I'm thinking about it. I hate guns but I know a lot of people who have had quite frightening experiences in LA and I'm glad I know how to shoot.'

But as well as bringing her to the attention of Hollywood casting agents, her part in *Passenger 57* also brought the beady eye of the US Immigration Department upon her. She claimed that she was forced to turn down starring roles in three films in 1992 because she wasn't deemed to have the proper papers. 'It changed the rules surrounding the immigration visas and for the time being I am not allowed to work,' she complained during a trip home to England that Christmas. 'It's very upsetting. I've really had some bad luck. But rules are rules and for the moment I have to obey them.' She calculated that the ban had cost her £630,000 in lost earnings and revealed that she had hired an attorney to sort things out. But the problems were not completely ironed out until March 1993, and only then after she had spent an entire day at the American Embassy in London.

Because of the visa red tape, Elizabeth was not able to capitalize fully on her success in *Passenger 57*. Neither could she console herself with the knowledge that she was about to star in one of British television's major new programmes. *Lady Chatterley's Lover* was a controversial subject and the certain furore surrounding its dramatization by the equally notorious Ken Russell would have guaranteed Elizabeth maximum exposure in the Press. But in the end even Russell's effusive praise was not enough to secure her the part. Problems with funding had delayed the production for over a year and by the time it finally got under way the much-coveted role was given to Joely Richardson.

The choice of Vanessa Redgrave's willowy daughter came as a huge surprise to everyone and even Richardson's agent had thought Elizabeth was favourite for the role. 'I've no idea why they didn't choose Elizabeth Hurley after all,' they said. 'She just didn't get it.' The hitherto little-known actor Sean Bean was picked to play the gamekeeper Mellors. Missing out on such a plum role was a bitter disappointment for Elizabeth, a blow made doubly hard to bear given her problems in America. It was also a huge embarrassment for it is every actor's nightmare to declare publicly that a role has been landed, only to lose the part to someone else. Elizabeth felt the humiliation keenly and although Hugh Grant did his best to be supportive, the disappointment was trebled when the series became a massive success and made household names of Richardson and Bean.

In October 1991, 10 months after she had left Hugh Grant behind in London to make her home in Los Angeles, Elizabeth was asked in a newspaper interview if she had ever felt tempted to cheat on him. Insisting that she had remained loyal, she replied, 'I have honestly not met anyone else. Neither do I have romances on film sets, although I see it happen all the time. I would never want Hugh to be in a position where people would laugh at him. I have been in situations when actors have been having affairs and then the wife or husband turns up. You have to be terribly nice to the regular partner, but all the time you are thinking, "If only you knew what was really happening."' She repeated her loyal declarations in an interview with *The Sun* the following January, saying, 'I haven't come across anybody I'm more attracted to than Hugh and I wouldn't cheat on him.'

But within months of making that remark, Elizabeth was embroiled in a passionate affair with another man. And so brazenly open was she about it that Hugh Grant was indeed being laughed at. Often separated from Hugh, it was perhaps inevitable that she would eventually succumb to infidelity. He was loath to spend any more time than he absolutely had to in Los Angeles and when he was in the city he refused to stay at Julia Verdin's house. It was thus usually left to Liz to make the tiring 12-hour journey back to London, trips financed by Hugh who generally paid for her airline ticket. During such visits she would take the opportunity to stock up on the things she missed from home, such as crumpets, Marmite and chocolate, but the visits could only do so much to shore up the couple's long-distance love affair. Sometimes they would manage to find time to snatch a holiday together, skiing in Austria or surfing in Cornwall, but the visits were often brief. During one trip to London in early 1993 the couple was only together for five days before Liz jetted back to Los Angeles to start work on a TV series called *The Resurrector* and Hugh headed for Australia to film his latest movie, *Sirens*.

Hugh would be working with the supermodel Elle Macpherson on *Sirens*, 'and a crowd of other raving beauties so I hate to think that he's up to,' Liz told the *Mail on Sunday*. But as she uttered those very words, she was keeping a guilty secret herself. She was in the throes of a highly charged sexual affair with her fellow 'Vile' William Annesley and the couple's relationship was to cause major ructions among the British ex-pat community in Los Angeles.

While Elizabeth was busy telling the *Daily Mail* how much she missed Hugh, and how his 'transatlantic cuddles' helped her cope when she became homesick, she was at the same time busy sleeping with Annesley. This was despite the fact that he was the boyfriend of her supposed best friend, Charlotte Lewis. But Birgit Cunningham recalls how the upper-crust Annesley never stood a chance against Liz's powers of seduction. 'Liz and I were sitting round the house one day reading magazines when Will rang the doorbell,' she says. 'Elizabeth leapt up in a panic and raced upstairs, telling me to let him in. We waited, and after

about four minutes down came Elizabeth in this sexy 1950s
negligee. It was a really outrageous little number with baby
goose feathers, and our mouths just dropped. Liz then did this
over-acted yawn and said, "I have just been taking the most
glorious nap."' And then she walked carefully towards him, like
a snake about to pounce. And she looked at me as if to say, "You
can leave now."'

A year younger than Elizabeth, William Annesley had had the
sort of upbringing that Elizabeth herself had aspired to. He
attended top public school Ludgrove, along with his friend
Henry Dent-Brocklehurst, and then went to Harrow. He says
that his ancestors used to own castles in Ireland, and his family
home was in that bastion of Ye Olde England, Stow-on-the-Wold,
Gloucestershire. He was good-looking, in the same English
public school way as Hugh Grant, and, most crucially of all, he
was mad about Elizabeth. Annesley had to keep his trysts with
Liz a secret, not least because he had a girlfriend, but he knew
that the chances of bumping into Hugh Grant were minimal.
'Hugh didn't like going to the house because there were always
too many people there,' he says today. 'Hugh likes the pub and
the quiet English life, whereas Julia's was always a big party. It
was like a who's who of Hollywood.' Whenever they had
arranged to meet, Annesley would drive to Julia Verdin's house,
park his car and, after making sure that no one was around,
scramble up and over the wall surrounding the house.

Their affair went on for six months but while carrying on like
the Milk Tray man may have suited Annesley, it was not enough
for Elizabeth. Not content with the secret knowledge that she
was having an affair with Annesley, she wanted others to know

too – especially Charlotte. Although they were supposed to be friends the highly competitive Elizabeth could not resist rubbing her pal's nose in it. Charlotte, who had starred with Eddie Murphy in the movie *Coming to America*, was well aware that the pair fancied each other, however she did not realize that they had actually done anything about it. Will had – rather foolishly – admitted to his girlfriend that he 'wouldn't mind knowing what Liz's body is like' and she told him she would find out for him. During a get-together at Julia Verdin's house, Annesley watched spellbound as Charlotte took Liz by the hand and led her into the bedroom, closing the door behind them. Will and two of his friends followed, absolutely fascinated. They were hammering on the door and clamouring to be allowed to watch, but the door stayed firmly closed for about 20 minutes. When they finally emerged, the women apparently had 'wicked smiles' on their faces.

'In all probability they were probably painting their toenails and having a good old laugh at how stupid one was,' says Annesley. Certainly Charlotte later insisted it had all been an act. 'William wanted me to have sex with Elizabeth while he watched,' she said. 'I only did it to please him because I'm not gay and neither is Elizabeth. We just went through the motions. I think she probably did it for William's sake as well because she had the big hots for him.' Things were to take a more serious turn, however, at a Viles dinner party. Elizabeth, seated opposite Annesley, began suggestively licking ice cream off a spoon while gazing directly at him. He went a guilty red and every one of the 15 people at the table could see what was going on, including Charlotte. 'She was really flirting with him at the dinner party and I have quite a volatile, passionate temper so I was getting more and more upset,' she says. Finally she could contain herself no longer and exploded in a rage. 'Why do you always have to fuck other people's boyfriends?' she screamed at Liz, before fleeing the room.

Undoubtedly part of the fun for Elizabeth was the kick she got from stealing Will Annesley from somebody else. 'She has got a bit of an evil streak,' says Birgit. 'She started a bit of a cat fight with Charlotte and I vaguely remember food being thrown at that dinner party. Charlotte went running out and Will went running after her and I remember looking at Liz and seeing this really wicked little grin on her face. I think she was enjoying it.'

Although she now strongly suspected that Liz was sleeping with her boyfriend, Charlotte did not know for sure until she made a devastating discovery in Will's bedroom. Climbing into his bed one day, she found a pair of Elizabeth's pyjamas – the damning proof that they had both betrayed her. Heartbroken and furious, she vowed to get her own back on Liz, and did so in spectacular style. Figuring that the one person who could put an end to the relationship was Hugh Grant, she packaged up the pyjamas and had them delivered to him on location in Australia. 'I really wanted to get some kind of revenge back so I sent them Federal Express to Hugh, with a note asking him to please stop his girlfriend fucking my boyfriend,' she says. 'It apparently did the trick. I am sure it was Will's fault as well as hers but at the time I was really in love with him so I was very hurt. Liz and I were friends and it devastated me.'

But where they had any feelings on the subject at all, most people's sympathies lay with Hugh Grant. Not many people felt that sorry for Charlotte because both she and Liz had a reputation for being notorious flirts. 'They are as bad as each other,' one Hollywood socialite has stated. 'Liz is not a girl's girl and neither is Charlotte. You wouldn't trust your boyfriend alone with either one of them.'

Birgit Cunningham admits that Liz enjoyed the power she exerted over men. 'We used to go out on the town trying to pull other girls' boyfriends,' she laughs. 'We were witches! It was so easy because the American girls had no idea how to make an entrance, how to enter a room or how to dress. At that time in the mid-1990s the girls in LA weren't interested in designer clothes.' The three English women, however, adored clothes and had the valuable advantage of having Elizabeth Emanuel as a friend. Emanuel, who together with her husband David had designed Princess Diana's wedding dress in 1981, often visited Verdin's home and was very generous with her creations. 'Elizabeth Emanuel would come over and stay with us quite a lot and lend us lots of lovely clothes,' says Birgit.

But if they considered their American sisters to be sadly lacking in the sartorial stakes, the women were even less impressed with their men. 'We weren't that interested in American men, they had to be well travelled or well read for us to be interested in them,' admits Birgit. 'They didn't know what to make of us with our designer labels and it was quite obvious that if you weren't the head of a studio or a big actress, American guys just weren't going to be interested. I had one or two dates with guys out there but I was just a secretary and there was always going to be some gorgeous model from Texas who would take them away. The idea of having a conversation with a girl beyond ten minutes just completely depressed them and a lot of those American girls would just do anything if you bought them a Diet Coke. You had to buy us lots of dinners before we'd even consider it, but most of the girls in LA are such complete and utter sluts that forget it: you couldn't compete with that.'

Rumours were rife among the ex-pats in Hollywood that William Annesley wasn't the only man Liz was sleeping with. 'I think it was a mischievous thing with Liz more than anything else,' defends Birgit. 'She was up for the game of the whole thing but I don't think she ever quite went through with it. As far as I know Will Annesley was the only one she had an affair with. She may well have loved him – Charlotte was in love with him so there must have been something about the guy.'

But there was also talk that Liz was having an affair with the wild American actor Tom Sizemore, who in 1995 starred in the movie *Heat*. Sizemore fanned the flames of the rumour mill by saying of Liz, 'She's a sexy, wonderful girl.'

To Elizabeth's horror, William Annesley was subsequently to kiss and tell on her, describing in intricate detail how he would shin up her balcony like some sort of Romeo figure to enjoy 'secret sex and spanking sessions' with the 'insatiable' Elizabeth. He would later profess to feel great shame over his actions, but that did not stop him from selling his story again in 2000, netting a further £30,000 from the *News of the World*. On that occasion he described how while Hugh Grant was away working to earn the 'giant cheques' to pay Liz's living expenses, she would be stripping to a tiny red bra and knickers for 'lust-filled' sessions with him. 'She's supple and athletic and what she doesn't know about sex isn't worth knowing,' he was quoted as saying. 'She'd wear me out. I owe her a debt of gratitude.' The article went on to describe the Mills and Boon-style seduction scene of his Hollywood apartment. 'I remember every moment,' Annesley chirped. 'We were drinking Veuve Cliquot champagne out of Waterford crystal glasses and Vivaldi was playing on the CD.' He 'tentatively' slipped an arm around her waist before leading his prize to the bedroom, which was lit – of course – by 'dozens of flickering candles'.

On and on went the indiscretions. Liz enjoyed being spanked, he said, and what's more, she liked to spank him too. She had 'fabulous breasts', 'the tiniest waist' and 'luminous' skin. 'It was a relationship based on lust,' he gossiped. 'What we had wasn't based on talk or shared interests.' However, by the time of writing, Annesley was in full shamefaced mode. 'It was an instant attraction on my part because she is gorgeous,' he says, speaking exclusively for this book. 'But I deeply regret what I did and I'm ashamed of it. It would be easy to offer up excuses but put it this way, one was not thinking straight. One knows right from wrong, and inherently I knew that it was not the act of a gentleman. It is something that I have to live with.' Guilty of that most unforgivable of crimes – talking to the Press for money – he was cast out by the Viles and cold-shouldered by many of Elizabeth's friends.

By July 1993, it was marriage and commitment that was on Elizabeth's mind, although sadly not for herself and Hugh. Her sister was getting married and Liz flew home to be her brides-maid. Kate, who was by now aged 29 and working as a writers' agent in London, married genealogist Daniel Curran in a cere-mony near her home in Wandsworth, south London. Kate revealed that Liz had been a very hands-on bridesmaid, ringing her up every minute of the day with ideas for the wedding dress, which Liz designed. 'The fact that I'm in London and she's in Los Angeles doesn't put her off,' Kate told the *Daily Mail*. 'And she usually phones when I'm asleep.' Her sister's nuptials inevitably led to renewed speculation as to when Liz and Hugh might make it down the aisle.

'They are conducting their romance by phone mostly at the moment,' Kate confided to the *Mail*. 'But if they decided to marry we'd all think it was great. I would love to have Hugh as a brother-in-law. I absolutely adore Hugh, but it's a strange thing because I can't imagine them getting married. Having said that, I can't imagine them not being together either.' But Liz maintained that they were both far too busy to tie the knot. 'Hugh's working like crazy,' she said. 'He's a manic wreck. But as for us getting wed, it's just too difficult with our work commitments and geographical separation.'

Hugh, she said, was busy working on a new film called *Four Weddings and a Funeral*, while she would be making a film in London. But as Grant was filming the role that would turn him into a worldwide star, Elizabeth's movie would turn her into a laughing stock. The problems with her work permit ongoing, she funded her LA lifestyle by filming low-budget movies in Europe. *Beyond Bedlam*, the 1993 film in which she played a mad scientist in charge of a mental asylum, was to go down in cinema history as one of the all-time stinkers.

Even the film's director, Vadim Jean, admitted it was a disaster. 'I really thought that I could turn the worst script in the world into something that was worth watching, and I thought as well that I could get a performance out of anybody,' he said. 'Sadly I was wrong.' The film was a flop and was denied a video release because it was deemed too violent. But those who did see it could not believe Elizabeth's spectacularly wooden acting. 'There was an amusing scene where she meets Craig Fairbrass and she seems to be doing the walk straight out of Monty Python's ministry of silly walks,' noted Matt Mueller, editor of *Total Film* magazine. 'She was either physically hobbled or she was attempting to climb a very steep staircase.'

Elizabeth was indeed walking in a bizarre manner in the film, her passion for high heels leading her to come a cropper. 'I told her at the beginning that the boots were not going to be any good,' revealed Vadim Jean. 'If you are wrestling with a burnt zombie corpse you can't wear high heels because it will all end in tears.' Jean was proved right when Elizabeth stumbled in her killer heels and sprained an ankle. 'Even though that happened, and it was terrible because she really hurt her ankle, she kept going,' he said. 'She was a complete trouper all the way to the end of the film. She never complained, she just mucked in. And that's Elizabeth. Absolutely determined to wear the high heels and absolutely determined to carry on even though she had sprained her ankle.'

But when he viewed the finished product, the director was appalled by what he saw. 'We saw the rushes and saw this kind of Quasimodo loping along, attempting to deliver these impossible-to-deliver lines,' he cringed. He also revealed how Elizabeth took great delight in winding up her famously volatile co-star Keith Allen. 'Keith was crawling through offal from an abattoir, bones and stuff and gallons of fake blood on the floor,' he explained. 'If you are the actor on the wrong side of the camera you deliver the best performance you can in order to help the other actor. That's what you do if you're being generous. Keith was screaming, "I'm going to get you," but Liz just looked bored and said, "Yes, I'm very, very scared." She was literally doing what we call marking out her lines. And I have to say that I made sure I walked with Keith up the corridor at the end of shooting because I thought he was going to hit her. I thought, "There's no question, he's going to smack her one."' Allen wasn't the only one to be annoyed by Elizabeth's attitude during the making of the film. The producer Paul Brooks was reportedly on the receiving end of what Hugh Grant described as Liz's 'legendary temper' when he got an unwelcome phone call on Christmas Day from Elizabeth, 'screaming and shouting' to get her own way.

By the beginning of 1994 Liz's career was not really going anywhere and she had not become the star she wanted to be. But a movie première and a few safety pins would shortly change all that ...

5 That Dress

A natural in front of the cameras, Elizabeth was a dream subject for photographers. Like *The Sunday Times* snapper who had required three sessions with her before he was content, Fleet Street's predominantly male photographers were universally captivated by the knockout combination of her fresh-faced beauty and voluptuous body. Top celebrity photographer John Stoddart was no exception. 'She just had this air of confidence about her,' he explains. 'But it wasn't an arrogant confidence because she was always very funny. The combination of her gorgeous good looks and this witty confident girl was fantastic. She was a classic English girl.'

Like many young actresses of her day, Elizabeth yearned to be treated like the glamorous film stars of yesteryear. In early 1994 Stoddart was asked to take a set of pictures of her and he decided to shoot them in black and white, as if they were for one of the sophisticated magazines like *Vanity Fair*. When he met her on the day of the shoot he was instantly struck by her looks. Elizabeth, he realized, was that rare kind of girl: one who really could stop traffic. As the pair prepared to cross London's busy Abbey Road, Liz brought drivers screeching to a halt. 'She had a tiny little white dress on, really tight, and she just put her foot on the road and the entire Abbey Road stopped,' he recalls. 'It was brilliant.'

Elizabeth positively smouldered in Stoddart's photographs, wearing sexy lingerie and displaying the blend of English rose and sultry sex siren that was to become her trade-mark. The pictures were subsequently bought by Tim Southwell, co-founder of a new men's magazine that was about to be launched on an unsuspecting public. Designed to appeal to 16- to 30-year-olds, the type of guys who enjoyed looking at pictures of near naked women but were reluctant to buy top shelf magazines, *Loaded* was the forerunner in a new wave of men's publishing. Often accused of being soft porn dressed up as lifestyle, it became the standard bearer for the lad culture of the 1990s. Within a few years there was scarcely a female soap star, singer or TV presenter who hadn't stripped down to her bra and panties for its front cover, but it was Elizabeth who was to have the distinction of being the first *Loaded* girl.

Southwell was extremely excited by Stoddart's raunchy photographs of Elizabeth, and when he spoke to her a few days later he was equally impressed by way she sounded. 'I was interviewing her on the phone in America and she had this quintessential English rose voice,' he says. 'I was looking at the pictures on my desk and listening to her talking to me and thinking, "Christ, this woman is absolutely sensational." There is nothing more exciting for a working-class lad like myself than to be confronted with a posh girl with a slightly slutty look who looks like she means business.'

The photos duly graced the magazine's debut edition in

April 1994 and immediately became a talking point. But it was neither Elizabeth's beauty nor Stoddart's expertise behind the lens that set tongues wagging – it was the spectacular absence of any air-brushing. Neither was it simply a matter of the magazine neglecting to air-brush out a pimple or blemish, it was far, far worse. 'The really remarkable thing about it was that you could see on either side of her gusset these great tufts of pubic hair,' explained journalist Toby Young incredulously. 'It was just unheard of.'

A more experienced model would have taken steps to ensure her bikini line stood up to such close scrutiny, but Elizabeth was sufficiently naïve not to have given it a thought. Equally, an experienced magazine picture desk would have routinely rectified the matter prior to publication. But the combination of Elizabeth's gaucherie and the magazine's infancy led to them being published in all their untouched-up glory. 'Most people would imagine that the *Loaded* staff would have known about air-brushing and the modern techniques of publishing, but I can assure you it was like the Double Deckers taking over a supersonic jet,' says Southwell. 'We didn't really know what was going on.'

While Elizabeth had been trying her hand at modelling, Hugh Grant's career was taking off big time. Excitement had been building over his new film, *Four Weddings and a Funeral*, since the previous summer and by the time Elizabeth's photos hit the streets in *Loaded* magazine Hugh was a big star. The film had a shoestring budget of just £3.75 million and as a result everyone pulled out the stops to get it made in only 36 days. According to Grant's biographer Jody Tresidder, he was ill for much of the breakneck-paced shoot, suffering from a mixture of nervousness, exhaustion and hay fever. She also says that he felt under enormous pressure from the film's exacting director Mike Newell. But as he and Liz took a much-needed holiday together that summer, they were cheered by increasingly encouraging bulletins about the finished product.

The film company had arranged a marathon publicity tour for *Four Weddings and a Funeral* in America, where it would be opening first. But before the US première, scheduled for April 1994, they decided to show it at the prestigious Sundance Film Festival in Utah. The festival, founded by Robert Redford as a showcase for small, independently produced films, was an American version of Cannes and a respected benchmark by which movies were judged. *Four Weddings* was shown there in January 1994 and received a rapturous response from the attending movie executives and film reviewers. Hugh Grant was quickly the name on everyone's lips and even Redford himself made time in his busy schedule to meet him. Hugh later joked that the legendary star had virtually ignored him during their lunch meeting, preferring to spend most of the meal chatting to Elizabeth.

With Hugh's other film, *Sirens*, also being premièred at the festival, it was very much his time. Elizabeth was there merely to provide moral support and keep him company. *Four Weddings* went down so well, not just at the festival but also at a series of carefully selected test screenings in the US, that it was decided to release it a whole month early. Within a month, it was number one at the US box office and Hugh had become an international star. The film was subsequently released in forty countries, topping box offices worldwide and earning more than £180 million. When it opened in cinemas across Britain two months later, it became the highest-attended movie ever, but that fact was to become almost lost among the reams of newspaper coverage generated by its momentous London première. It had been planned as a major event by the movie's publicity department, with the Odeon, Leicester Square, decorated like a church, complete with full choir, and the three thousand strong crowd outside supplied with confetti to throw at the stars as they arrived. But as the PRs were fine-tuning the arrangements for the big night, Elizabeth was masterminding a grand scheme of her own.

As Hugh's girlfriend, she was naturally planning to attend the première with him. And aware that all eyes would be upon them as they arrived, she realized it was the perfect opportunity for her to project herself into the limelight too. Determined, as ever, to be the centre of attention, she sought out an outfit that would render every other woman invisible on the night. Her bid to hijack the attention away from the film's true stars was to be spectacularly successful, earning herself a place in modern history as the perpetrator of some of the most outrageous scene-stealing exhibitionism ever witnessed.

On the eve of the première in May 1994, Toby Young called round to see his friend at her London flat. 'Liz had just flown in from LA and she answered the door wearing the smallest dress I had ever seen,' he recalls. 'When I walked in she stood in front of a mirror, thrust her breasts outward and asked me, "What do you think of this?" I said, "The paparazzi will love it." She said, "I'm not worried about them, it's Hugh's mum I'm worried about."' The dress Elizabeth was wearing was a £2,500 black silk couture evening dress made by the flamboyant Italian designer Gianni Versace – master of outrageously sexy dressing. It had been loaned to her specially for the première, and as well as a daringly plunging front, it was held together at the sides by two dozen giant gold safety pins. It was classic Versace: glamorous in a tacky, show-business way and absolutely guaranteed to make any woman wearing it stand out in a crowd. On Liz Hurley's voluptuous frame it was a total knockout, sending people's chins crashing to the ground at the very sight of her. She chose to accessorize it simply, with gold hoop earrings and the world's hottest male movie star on her arm.

When Elizabeth stepped out on to the red carpet on Hugh Grant's arm at the première on May 12, hundreds of flashbulbs popped as the gasping photographers captured her sensational arrival. The resulting photographs showed a ravishing young woman, smiling broadly and displaying ample creamy white bosom. Men all over Britain fell in love with her on the spot. To the average red-blooded male, she was a breath of fresh air. Here, at last, was a woman who looked real, who had boobs and curvy hips and wasn't afraid to enjoy her sexuality. In stark contrast to the brittle, aloof beauty of Hollywood actresses and supermodels, Liz looked refreshingly approachable – like an exceptionally pretty barmaid on a night out.

At the after-show party, held at the Naval and Military Club in Piccadilly, Liz positively shone, secure in the knowledge that her appearance had been a triumph. She had just pulled off the greatest role of her career. 'There was a deathly hush when everyone saw her, and then all the photographers went completely mental,' said Liz and Hugh's delighted PR Stacey

Wood. Julia Short, the PR for Polygram Films, was also beside herself with joy. 'Everybody was completely gobsmacked,' she said happily. 'It looked sensational, although for the life of me I can't work out how she got it on or how it stayed on.' The dress – a perfect size 10 – had made its first high-profile outing with the Danish model Helena Christiansen on the Milan catwalk, but once Elizabeth had worn it that was soon forgotten. 'The dress walked around the party and everyone was looking at it,' said Julia Short. 'And they were all saying, "Who is she?"'

In the face of such enormous competition, the other women present figured that they may as well go home. The infamous exhibitionist Paula Yates, one of many celebrity guests at the party, didn't even bother to remove the denim jacket covering her own skimpy party outfit. 'The other femme fatales didn't even try to compete,' said top paparazzo Dave Bennett. 'Wearing it was a brilliant tactical move because everyone else was dressed in white, as if for a wedding. It was a total showstopper.' There were a few bitchy remarks about the dress being 'over the top', but these came almost exclusively from women. 'She looked stunning but there was some negative muttering and whispering going around,' said Sky TV presenter Tania Bryer. 'She obviously thought she was going to make this one a big one. No one wears Versace unless they want to make a huge statement. He is not the master of subtlety.' And when Emma Freud, the girlfriend of *Four Weddings and a Funeral*'s script writer Richard Curtis, spoke to Liz at the party she gasped, 'Oh, my God. I've come as a bride and you've come as a mistress.'

Michael Foster, the head of ITN, asked Elizabeth if she realized that every woman in the room hated her for wearing the dress, only to be corrected by another guest who said, 'No, they hate you for being able to wear it.'

The next morning's papers were full of Elizabeth's sensational appearance. She even managed to knock the news of the premature death of Labour leader John Smith off the front pages, and the film's British actress, Kristen Scott Thomas, received scarcely a mention. Despite the fact that she had no part in the film, Elizabeth had nonetheless managed to make herself a part of its success. But nobody, she least of all, could have imagined just how big an impact the safety-pin dress would have on her career. Overnight she went from being a struggling minor actress to a major star. 'It was unprecedented for a starlet to use a movie première as a shop window in which to advertise her charms by wearing an incredibly revealing dress,' said Toby Young. 'That subsequently became a trend.'

Liz was later to claim that the dress was something she had just happened to throw on at the last minute, but freelance Fleet Street photographer Dave Hogan reveals that he and his colleagues had been tipped off that she would be wearing something spectacular. 'There were rumours it was going to be something special on the evening and it was,' he says. 'When she got out of the car there was a great uproar of, "Wow!" She stole the show and I'm sure at the end of the evening they sat back and said, "Job well done."' Sure enough, it emerged that the Versace office in London had received a phone call from Elizabeth's agent a full month beforehand, telling them that she was looking for something stunning to wear for the première. But when she arrived at the designer's Bond Street shop she could not find anything suitable – until the PR assistant remembered a dress that was hanging in the corner of the Press Office. The dress was duly produced and when Liz slipped it on, it was a perfect fit. 'Because this dress leaves so little to the imagination, you have to be confident and have an amazing body to wear it,' said a Versace spokesman. 'Liz was the perfect person.'

'That dress', as it came to be known, was destined to become just as famous as its wearer. It was flown back to Milan the morning after the première, where it was permanently ensconced in Versace's museum archive. By the time similar dresses arrived in the London store they had been modified to be less blatantly sexy. Even so, all six sold within two hours, despite the £2,500 price tag. The dress also spawned a thousand high street imitations as women up and down the country sought to emulate Elizabeth's sex appeal. And during the BBC's 1995 Comic Relief fundraiser, television viewers bid an unprecedented £1 million to watch tubby comedienne Dawn French – clad in an outsize version of the dress – energetically French kiss a hapless Hugh Grant.

Within days of the *Four Weddings* première, there was scarcely a newspaper reader in the land who could have been unaware of who Elizabeth Hurley was. The good people of Basingstoke were particularly riveted – she was after all the town's first bona fide 'celebrity', easily eclipsing its previously best-known daughter, the gloomy singer Tanita Tikaram. But among her former acquaintances, opinions were divided as to whether Liz had emerged from the mêlée well. Aileen Scriven, who knew Liz at the Amateur Theatrical Society, considered that she was selling herself short by presenting herself as a glamorous appendage to Hugh Grant. 'I knew she was going to do something because she had got the looks and everything else to go with it, but I didn't expect her to appear on the arm of somebody wearing next to nothing,' she says. 'I don't disapprove, but if somebody had said to me that was what she was going to do, I wouldn't have believed it.'

Old college friend Derek Thompson disagreed. 'Liz is a strong person and when you saw her on Hugh Grant's arm she was definitely no accessory,' he says. And *Tatler* editor Jane Proctor argued that Liz had actually helped to raise Hugh Grant's profile rather than the other way round. 'He never made it on to the front pages of the tabloids before she appeared with him in that Versace dress,' she pointed out.

Acres of newsprint were subsequently devoted to glowing articles about Liz, prompting the *Observer* to compare her to Aphrodite herself. 'The obsession with both women speaks to an age-old human need to kneel down before the beautiful ... and gibber adoration,' it said. 'Cavemen knelt before the stars or the darkness of the solar eclipse; the ancient Greeks were held rapt by tales about the beauty of Aphrodite; today Fleet Street writes fawning rubbish about Elizabeth Hurley.' Liz had to endure the odd nasty remark in the Press – such as the *Daily Mail* fashion editor's observation that her legs were 'more High Street than high fashion', but on the whole she was enjoying a mutually rewarding love affair with the media. This was to be short-lived, however, as she discovered fame was a double-edged sword. The backlash began almost immediately with the John Stoddart photographs she had so willingly posed for before Hugh's meteoric rise to superstardom now coming back to haunt her.

Toby Young, who was at that time the editor of literary

magazine *Modern Review*, was another male who had been captivated by Elizabeth. He praised her in the magazine for being 'chummy, plummy and yummy'. 'Her sexiness is so upfront and guileless, it's almost innocent,' he gushed. 'She doesn't turn it on for the cameras like Sharon Stone. She's completely incapable of turning it off.' *Modern Review* was giving away audio books of Julie Burchill's sexually explicit novel *Ambition*, which Young had persuaded Liz to read. 'The idea of her wrapping her velvet voice around these Anglo-Saxon expletives, which the book is absolutely riddled with, seemed quite appealing,' he said. He had bought in the *Loaded* photographs to promote the talking book, and was also planning to use an as-yet-unseen shot of her topless.

When she found out what her supposed friend was up to, Elizabeth erupted in fury. 'The next thing I knew, I was getting a call from Elizabeth, and I think her opening gambit was, "Toby, you're a scumbag, a complete and utter scumbag,"' he stated. 'She was furious that I had decided to use the topless picture and I was completely baffled by this because although the topless picture hadn't appeared anywhere else, photographs from the same set had already appeared in *Loaded*, *Esquire* and *GQ* magazines. But now she was a bona fide, fully fledged celebrity she didn't want to tarnish this new wattage by having any more naked pictures appearing.' Young stood his ground but Elizabeth was equally determined that the pictures would not be used. The dispute ended their friendship and Elizabeth called in lawyers to scare him off. Threatened with legal action, *Modern Review* was forced to pulp 20,000 covers of the cassette. Unsurprisingly, Young was later to be rather less than flattering about his 'yummy' former pal. 'She had a steely quality, you could see behind the eyes that there was this shark-like determination to succeed,' he sniped.

May 1994 was to be the most eventful month of Elizabeth's life thus far. Her sister was expecting her first child, a happy prospect but one which provoked mixed emotions in Liz. 'At the moment she is being tortured with me being eight months pregnant,' Kate revealed. 'She is furious that I'm having children because her lifelong ambition was that we should have them at the same time. She's got an absolute horror that I might love the baby more than her.' Elizabeth wanted to be with her sister for the birth, a plan which Kate had agreed to, despite reservations. 'I've got this bet with myself as to how long the doctor will keep her in there before he kicks her out for barking instructions left, right and centre,' she worried.

With several weeks to go before the birth, Elizabeth was able safely to accompany Hugh to the South of France for the Cannes Film Festival later that month. There the couple was put up in style at the magnificent Hotel du Cap, luxuriating in true film-star splendour. One of them, at least, was a bona fide film star, taking phone calls from Hollywood movie directors and the international Press and sifting through the scripts that arrived by courier on a daily basis. They were staying in a £750-a-night suite, paid for by the film company, and getting used to the pampering that from then on would become a regular way of life. In July the couple was back in France, staying free at the equally luxurious Paris Ritz. But this time it was Elizabeth's cachet that had brought them the freebie. Her appearance in That Dress had done much to enhance Gianni Versace as a leading designer and it was he who paid to put them up at the Ritz. Liz and Hugh were VIP guests at the show to launch his latest collection – the first fashion show that Liz had ever been to.

Although she and Versace subsequently became friends, she admitted that she had never heard of him until she was loaned the safety-pin dress. And when the time came finally to meet him, she was inordinately nervous. 'I felt scruffy, schoolgirlish and unsophisticated and also very intimidated by the fashion world,' she wrote in *The Daily Telegraph* in 1999. 'Luckily, Gianni was absolutely heavenly: charming, easy, funny and silly.'

Although she was delighted by the attention that her appearance in That Dress had brought her, Elizabeth was not particularly pleased when she saw the photographs of herself wearing it. While the majority of men – and most women – saw a slim, healthy, curvaceous woman with an enviable figure, Liz fell victim to the insidious fashion industry dictum that women should be stick thin. 'She looked at the pictures and I think she probably had a different reaction than every hot blooded man in the country,' says Jane Proctor. 'She went, "Oh, gosh. I look fat."' Even before she began pursuing a career as an actress, Elizabeth had fretted about her weight. The days when she had read diet books and carried out the instructions in reverse had been short-lived and in her late teens she began her lifelong battle to be slim. 'She used to complain about how much she weighed,' says her friend Debra Holder. 'She would say, "I'm nine-and-a-half-stone now and I'm so peed off." She did try to lose weight but she had trouble at that age. She didn't eat much, which helped, but she always had a very fit body.'

After the *Four Weddings* première, Elizabeth immediately

resolved to lose weight. She had a big incentive to help her as she had been invited to appear on the front cover of *Tatler* – a prestigious accolade that most actresses would give their right arm for. 'Early on she didn't warrant a cover but after the Versace safety pin dress moment I think she could have asked for a cover on virtually any magazine,' says Jane Proctor. 'She spent a month grooming herself and suddenly, there in front of us, was this fully formed Hollywood superstar. She looked so beautiful, so polished, so poised and the resulting pictures were absolutely fantastic.'

Elizabeth, 15 pounds lighter, did indeed look sensational and it was the highest-selling edition in the magazine's 285-year history. She was on a roll, and lucky break led to lucky break. Being Hugh Grant's girlfriend had enabled her to attend the *Four Weddings* première; her appearance in That Dress had caused *Tatler* to put her on their front cover; and being in the magazine would soon lead to her finding a new career as an international model.

That Dress may have turned Liz into a star in Britain, but in America neither she nor the dress had caused any ripples. 'It didn't make any news out here,' says Birgit Cunningham. 'We only got *Variety* and the *Hollywood Reporter* at the house and there was nothing about Liz Hurley in either of them. I remember seeing a copy of the *Daily Mail* on the table with a picture of Liz but I didn't think anything of it. Julia told me that Liz had had to handle a lot of press back in London, but I had no idea how much sensation it had caused. Life carried on.'

Now that he had proved himself as leading man material, Hollywood film companies were falling over themselves to get

Hugh to appear in their films. Castle Rock, the studio financed by American movie mogul Ted Turner, was sufficiently keen to have him on their books that they were prepared to let him call the shots and commission his own movie projects, provided that they got first refusal. Hugh and Elizabeth were quick to capitalize on this and in October 1994 they set up their own production company, Simian Films Ltd – named as an in-joke reference to their obsession with monkeys. The pair subsequently explained to anyone who asked that the name – meaning ape-like – had been inspired by Elizabeth's opinion that Hugh looked like a monkey. 'If you look very carefully, you'll notice his ears are too small and too high on his head,' she said. 'That gives him a very simian look.'

Hugh was being hailed on both sides of the Atlantic as 'the new Cary Grant' and was even being tipped as the next James Bond. The makers of *Sirens* could not believe their luck. They had hired a little-known actor for a modest fee but now had themselves an accredited Hollywood movie star. Until that point they had been relying on the naked Elle Macpherson as the film's main selling point but with Hugh suddenly projected to superstardom the PR department hurriedly repackaged their campaign to push him as the major attraction.

Although it was American actress Andie MacDowell and Kristen Scott Thomas who were Hugh's co-stars in *Four Weddings and a Funeral*, it had been Elizabeth who benefited the most publicity-wise from the film's London opening. And accompanying him to the British première of *Sirens* at the end of July, she could not resist once again hogging the limelight. In the face of daunting competition in the form of Aussie supermodel

Macpherson, Liz nonetheless succeeded in upstaging the film's actual stars. In what was becoming something of a trend for her, it was Elizabeth's face that appeared in the newspapers the following morning.

Fleet Street picture editors may have loved her for it, grateful for the fact that any event involving Liz was guaranteed to produce a sexy shot for the front page, but female columnists expressed nothing but contempt for her scene-stealing antics. 'It should have been Elle Macpherson's night. It was, after all, the première of a film in which she stars … Yet again however … our Liz could not bear the attention to rest with those who deserved it,' wrote the *Sunday People*'s Carol Sarler. She went on to chastise Liz for 'parading herself mercilessly in front of the photographers' and expressed her personal satisfaction that the *People* at least had not put Liz on their front page that week.

While she enjoyed the attention of photographers at premières and liked seeing herself plastered over the front pages, Elizabeth did not enjoy the tabloids' enthusiastic, full-scale investigations into her past. Old friends were sought out and her heyday as the Punk Queen of Basingstoke revealed. Her colourful reputation as a teenage rebel made for good copy and Liz was in the papers almost every day. Far more so than her boyfriend, in fact – to Hugh Grant's blessed relief. Actor David Thewlis, who was working with Hugh on his subsequent film *Restoration*, was quoted as saying, 'Each time you open the papers, it's like the Daily Hurley.' It wasn't just the tabloids either: the traditionally sober broadsheets were equally captivated, prompting the satirical magazine *Private Eye* to do a full-page spoof of 'The Daily Hurleygraph'.

Liz sought to control publicity by courting it on her own terms. While she wished to forget about the *Loaded* pictures and had taken legal action to stop *Modern Review* from using them, she did agree to pose in *The Sunday Times* – naked save for a strategically placed feather boa. She also appeared on the front cover of its magazine supplement, wearing a skimpy lilac shirt, high heeled-leather boots and revealing a smooth expanse of bare buttock. In the accompanying interview she complained about Toby Young's 'outrageous behaviour' and sanctioned her friend Henry Dent-Brocklehurst to talk about the 'real Elizabeth'. Brocklehurst obediently divulged how Elizabeth had put him up at her flat while he was recovering from a broken heart, and how her kindness had sealed their friendship. She was, he intimated, almost like a mother to him and his fellow Viles. She came particularly into her own during their communal Sunday roast dinners in Los Angeles. 'She would always make an extra effort to make sure that the puddings were ready, that the custard was just the right temperature,' he praised gushingly.

The Los Angeles-based British reporters were also keen to know what Liz was up to – and who she might be up to it with. Rumours had been circulating for some time that she was not faithful to Hugh, rumours not helped by the couple's constant comments that they were like brother and sister. As the partner of a major star, not to mention a darling of the British tabloids in her own right, Liz's every move was of major interest. 'We started to get phone calls in the middle of the night, and of course I assumed it was Hugh Grant trying to send a fax,' says Birgit. 'I remember one time answering the phone at about four in the morning and being really panicked that it might be bad news about my family, but it turned out to be a journalist asking about Liz. I mentioned it the next morning and Julia said she'd had a phone call as well.' Birgit still had little idea why anyone would want to know things about her flatmate but Liz soon put her in the picture.

However, instead of simply advising her friend to say 'no comment' and put the phone down, Liz made the whole scenario appear like something out of a spy film. 'Liz and Julia sat me down and explained what was going on and told me I wasn't allowed to say anything on the phone and to keep an eye out in case people came in the door that we didn't know,' Birgit explains. 'They really got me quite nervous. They said, "People are going to be calling you in the night and we might have people climbing over the walls so we are going to put glass on the wall." It was quite scary because I didn't know anything about journalists. They explained that they were trying to get photos of Liz, and told me what to do and what not to do.'

Liz succeeded in making Birgit feel as if the house was truly under siege. 'One day I woke up early and discovered a guy in the kitchen who I didn't know,' she says. 'He had his shirt off and was covered in tattoos. He was making himself a cup of coffee. He looked really scary and I absolutely froze. I thought he might be some mad fan or something like that, so I crouched down and said, "Who are you and what are you doing here?" But he just started laughing at me and said, "And what are you going to do?" I thought about going for one of the kitchen knives, and I told him again to tell me who he was, because I knew he wasn't dating Julia or Liz. Eventually he told me that he was a friend of an actor who was crashing in one of the rooms. It turned out that he was Stephen Baldwin! I was so embarrassed.'

It wasn't the only misunderstanding caused by Liz's paranoia. 'Another time someone who was staying at the house forgot their key and broke in through my window,' says Birgit. 'I almost killed him. It was quite a big house and because friends of friends would call in you couldn't really keep track of what was going on. It was always a bit nerve-racking but I never did catch a journalist!' Ironically, Elizabeth subsequently decided to leave Julia Verdin's house and moved in with journalist William Cash. 'Hugh is very welcome to stay here whenever he wants,' said Cash, adding, somewhat oddly, 'There's a sofa bed downstairs.'

In marked contrast to Hugh Grant's acting career, Elizabeth's was idling in neutral. She was seen only fleetingly on British TV screens in 1994, cropping up in the summer as the wife of an English colonel in the Napoleonic War series *Sharpe*. The show starred Sean Bean as the swashbuckling hero, and gave Elizabeth, who had narrowly missed out on starring opposite him in *Lady Chatterley's Lover*, the opportunity at last to indulge in a bit of bodice-ripping with him. Once again she was topless, and once again her willingness to get her kit off for the cameras was a triumph. According to the *Daily Record*, a quick flash of the by-now-famous Hurley curves managed to draw in 10 million viewers to the show and power companies reported a 25 per cent electricity surge during the break. 'Around 500 megawatts were suddenly switched on during the ads,' stated the paper. 'That's well up on the 400 megawatts the week before when Liz and her boobs were out of sight.' Five hundred megawatts, its reporter helpfully explained, was equivalent to 300,000 kettles being turned on simultaneously.

Sean Bean, however, was not overly impressed by Liz's charms and in truth it would be hard to imagine the two of them ever hitting it off. A down-to-earth, football-loving, man's man from Sheffield, Bean had little in common with the pretentious and attention-seeking Elizabeth. 'He must be one of the most reluctant sex symbols I have ever met,' she said afterwards. 'He is charming and adorable but he is rather straight-laced.' In newspaper interviews to promote her role in *Sharpe*, Elizabeth admitted that she was envious of Hugh's fame. 'Hugh has got the break that everyone dreams of and I'm really pleased for him – if not a little bit jealous,' she said. 'Luckily the attention he is getting hasn't changed him for the worse, if anything he has become more humble. We are both enjoying the fact he is doing so well.'

But the difference between the couple's respective prospects as actors could not be more marked. While Hollywood was lobbing huge sums of money at Hugh Grant in the hope of recreating the magic of *Four Weddings and a Funeral*, Elizabeth's film *Beyond Bedlam* was famous only for being famously bad. Refused a video release, it quickly disappeared from the minds of all but the most idiosyncratic movie fan. 'The film is probably not everyone's cup of tea,' Liz acknowledged. 'I don't like violence myself but it's amusing that it's gained cult status.' Hugh put it more accurately – if unkindly – when he labelled the film 'unspeakable'. 'It was a chancre, I think we can safely say that,' he said. For the benefit of anyone languishing in blissful ignorance of what a chancre is, it is apparently an ulcer caused by venereal disease.

As her name became more and more well known, people began to question why exactly it was that Elizabeth had become so famous. It certainly wasn't for her acting skills – that much at least was glaringly obvious. So why were the papers so obsessed with Liz? 'It didn't really matter that she wasn't very good at anything, she was just there to be this symbol of glamour,' explains Tim Southwell. 'That combination of beauty, self-effacing humour, confidence and self esteem is dynamite.' An article in the *Observer* argued that the fact that she had few acting roles behind her was beside the point. 'She has become a true icon of female sexuality (TIFS) in a world that abounds with cheap imitations,' it said. 'She is very much her own invention [and] who is to say that to be a TIFS is more ignoble a way of earning a crust for a woman than, say, cornering the market in sanctimony as Esther Rantzen has done.' Liz, the article maintained, was a Lady Godiva of our times. 'Sneer away, those who would do her down,' it concluded.

But support for the 'lovely Liz' was becoming increasingly thin – much like her, actually. 'Am I missing something when papers go wild about Liz Hurley?' asked exasperated columnist Joe Haines in the now defunct *Today* newspaper. 'In her worst photos she reminds me of Virginia Bottomley. The late Ginger Rogers was class and didn't have to go half-naked to prove it.'

Both inevitably, and somewhat tediously for the couple, the subject matter of Hugh's hit film led to renewed speculation as to when they might marry. 'We have been inundated with people asking but you'll have to ask him. He's the star,' said Liz. In September Hugh got time off from filming *The Englishman Who Went Up a Hill and Came Down a Mountain* and they were able to have their first proper holiday together in two and a half years. Eschewing more glamorous destinations like the Maldives or the Caribbean, they opted for the peaceful charms of the West Country.

Driving down in Hugh's black Mercedes, the couple checked into the famous Seafood Restaurant in Padstow, Cornwall. The hotel, which is run by the TV chef Rick Stein, overlooks the harbour and is a favourite haunt of *bon viveurs* and celebrities. Hugh and Liz were looking forward to a week of country walks and surfing, but on their arrival the weather was atrocious. Pouring with rain, and with a distinctly wintry chill in the air, Liz must have thought longingly of the Californian sunshine. But showing the British aptitude for embracing the elements, she and Hugh donned dark green Barbour jackets and baseball caps and ventured out, even taking a rain-lashed boat trip across the bay.

That evening at dinner, the restaurant's well-heeled customers kept a discreet silence when Britain's most famous celebrity couple entered the room. Dressed in a black jumper, red tartan miniskirt and high heels, Elizabeth lent a distinctly metropolitan glamour to the restaurant. There was no doubting who either of them was, but their fellow diners politely pretended not to notice them, content to sneak occasional surreptitious glances in their direction. This was only good manners, of course, and Hugh Grant would no doubt have been extremely displeased to have his evening interrupted by star-struck autograph hunters. He maintained a low profile through dinner, speaking in a quiet voice and seldom raising his head to look around. But being so studiously ignored by the other customers did not suit Liz in the slightest, even if she was on holiday. While Hugh was telling her to order dessert, pointing out that they had, after all, paid for it, Elizabeth was planning a spot of attention-seeking. Her entrance had not raised any eyebrows, but she was determined that her exit would.

Pushing back her chair at the end of the meal, she walked slowly round behind the still-seated Hugh and leaned over his shoulders. Draping her arms around his neck and smiling seductively, she nuzzled his ear and let her hair cascade over his shoulder. Bending from the waist, she stuck her bottom in the air, treating the by now incredulous diners to the sight of her knickers. Hugh, who it has to be said did not look altogether comfortable about his girlfriend's antics, stood up and the two of them left the room. The minute they had gone, the restaurant erupted in a buzz of excited whispers. Elizabeth's little floor-show had had the desired effect.

The next day the weather had improved enough for the couple to go surfing. They drove along the coast towards the surfers' paradise of Newquay, stopping to hire boards from a surf shack along the way. Hugh, an experienced surfer, picked a small beach to introduce novice Liz to the sport. With his baseball cap on back to front and his jeans rolled up to the knees, he stood on the beach giving her instructions. Wearing a black wetsuit and with her hair in bunches, she took to the waves bravely but didn't stay in the chilly water for long. As they walked back up the beach, with Hugh carrying her surfboard, it was clear why she had caused such a sensation in That Dress. 'Her figure was amazing,' said an onlooker. 'She looked like a Bond girl.'

Back in the busy car park, however, Elizabeth was to cause even more of a stir. While Hugh valiantly tried to protect her modesty by holding a towel around her, she peeled off her wetsuit, making no attempt to stay behind the towel's screen. And when he went away to rinse her suit under a tap, she let the towel fall away completely, seemingly unconcerned that everyone in the car park could see that she was stark naked. Hugh came back and tried to hold the towel up again but Liz wrapped it round her top half, revealing a still naked bottom. Despite the cold weather she took her time getting dressed, standing around in a G-string and T-shirt as she slowly dried herself.

After a pub lunch the couple went for a walk at the appropriately named Booby Bay. Elizabeth kept her clothes on this time, wearing an oversized coat but with bare legs. Hand in hand, the couple was clearly enjoying a very romantic holiday. Back at the Seafood Restaurant that evening their bemused fellow hotel guests could hear her singing to Hugh in the bathroom as they got ready for dinner. 'Love me like a monkey,' she sang, bizarrely, accompanied by much splashing of water.

When Hugh returned to Wales to finish filming, Liz stayed in London where she had an appointment to switch on the Oxford Street Christmas lights in November. She had never felt particularly safe in Los Angeles, hence her membership of the Beverly Hills Gun Club and the lessons she'd taken in kick-boxing, but when she became a victim of a street robbery in November 1994, it was in one of London's most salubrious and safe neighbourhoods. She was walking home through Chelsea one evening, her mind no doubt on the glamorous party she was going to be attending that night at the jewellers Tiffanys, when she was pounced upon by four teenage thieves. One of her assailants held a knife to her throat and warned, 'Give us your money or I'll cut you.'

The story made newspaper headlines, not just because of Elizabeth's fame but because she was a victim of a frightening new phenomenon: the all-girl gang. Her assailants, two of whom were only 17, had spent the afternoon drinking cheap wine before deciding to rob someone. Faced with a six-inch knife, the terrified Liz handed them a £10 note from her handbag, only for one of the girls to complain, 'We can't even get some Big Macs with that.' But as she pushed the girls away and ran into the road, a passing motorist came to her aid. 'I saw something I didn't like and thought I had to step in,' said Sam Latifi, a 30-year-old van driver from Hendon, North London. 'A young lady was in a situation and obviously having difficulties. I had to go to help her. She wasn't screaming or crying but she was talking very fast and out of breath.'

When they saw the burly driver climbing out of his van, the girls ran off down the road. After handing Liz his mobile phone and telling her to call the police, Mr Latifi bravely took off in pursuit, getting himself threatened with the knife for his trouble. Elizabeth's saviour, hailed by *The Sun* newspaper as 'the UK's most envied white knight', was in blissful ignorance of who she was. 'During our chat I asked what she did and she told me she was an actress,' he said. 'I thought, "Poor thing, she must be out of work," because I did not recognize her.' A children's nanny who comforted Liz after the incident confessed that she didn't know who she was either. Joanna Brown, who watched the attack take place outside her window, invited

Elizabeth inside for some coffee. 'They were pushing her and hitting her and trying to get her bag,' she said. 'She was shouting "Get off me" and she looked like she was really in trouble. I called the police straight away and came out to see if she was OK. She was a bit shaken to start with but she calmed down very quickly. She was very brave.'

The girls were arrested at the scene and questioned at Chelsea police station. After giving a statement to the police, Elizabeth was driven home in an unmarked police car to the flat she shared with Hugh in Kensington. 'It was very frightening but I don't really want to talk about it,' she told waiting reporters. She managed a smile for the photographers but was clearly anxious to get inside to Hugh.

With not much work of her own to do, Elizabeth was able to accompany Hugh to the host of international film awards honouring *Four Weddings*. At the Golden Globe Awards in Los Angeles in January 1995, he was voted Best Comedy Actor and in his witty acceptance speech, which was received to rapturous applause, he paid touching tribute to Liz for tolerating his behaviour during the intense period of filming. She had, he said, 'put up with easily the nastiest, most ill-tempered, prima-donna-ish actor in English cinema for six weeks and then came back to me, which was really nice'.

But in March 1995 Elizabeth got the break that was to make her internationally famous in her own right. She landed the much-coveted contract to be the new face of the American cosmetics giant Estée Lauder – a job said to be worth a cool £2 million a year. 'Once you've got that under your belt, you know you've made it,' commented Clare Castagnetti, a director of the

175, Buckskin Avenue, Basingstoke, the bungalow where Liz grew up.

Harriet Costello School, Basingstoke, the comprehensive
she attended until the age of 16.

Liz, aged 13, playing Gretel in Basingstoke Amateur Theatrical Society's production of Hansel and Gretel. (*right and below*)

Liz, aged17, on the train to London to attend a punk concert.

Septic, aka Antony Allcock, Liz's first boyfriend.

Blondie: Punk queen Liz, aged 17, with a friend. (*above and below*)

Snakebite queen: Liz knocks back another pint of her favourite tipple - lager and cider mixed with blackcurrant.

That Dress: Liz with Hugh
at the London premiere of
*Four Weddings and a
Funeral* in the Versace
safety-pin dress that
started it all.

Liz and Hugh on a surfing and walking holiday in north Cornwall, summer 1994.

Shaming of a superstar: Hugh Grant's police mug shot following his arrest with a Californian hooker in June 1995.

Divine Brown, his partner in crime.

Liz shows off her post pregnancy curves while stepping out with her friends
Sir Elton John and his partner David Furnish.

Liz tells her side of the story of Hugh Grant's arrest to Barbara Walters on
America's ABC television. The interview made her a household name in the US.

Like father like son: Liz with baby Damian Charles Hurley (*right*), her son by Hollywood playboy Stephen Bing.

Liz and Steve Bing (*left*) before their relationship turned into one of the most bitter break-ups in recent times.

Select modelling agency. And according to Jane Proctor, it was all thanks to Elizabeth's appearance in *Tatler*. Estée Lauder had been looking for someone to replace supermodel Paulina Porizkova for some time, and as editor of one of the most influential magazines in the world, Proctor's opinion was duly sought. 'The rumour at the time was that the Princess of Wales had been approached, and several Hollywood actresses were in the frame,' Proctor explains. 'I said that our biggest-selling cover had been Elizabeth Hurley and I suggested her for the job.'

At the Press conference to announce the news, staged at the Manhattan's Royalton Hotel, Elizabeth positively shone. And this time it was Hugh who was standing by *her* side. To the Americans, Elizabeth was a fresh discovery: a poised, radiantly beautiful young woman who also happened to be the girlfriend of everyone's favourite English actor. Scores of journalists and photographers turned out for the Press conference and the event created the kind of media hysteria seldom seen since the days of Elizabeth Taylor and Richard Burton. It had always upset Elizabeth that she was seen as Hugh's appendage but now at last she had a status of her own. 'It gave her a handle,' said Toby Young. 'She could be referred to as Estée Lauder cover girl Elizabeth Hurley, but actually – objectively – it's kind of a step down. She was an actress and she became a supermodel. Usually the traffic is in the other direction.'

Later that month Elizabeth had to leave New York, where much of her Estée Lauder work was based, and return to London to give evidence in the trial of the women who had mugged her. Flying in on Concorde in true superstar style, she arrived at Southwark Crown Court on March 22 to face a battalion of fifty photographers. Wearing suitably starry dark glasses, black jacket and tight black leggings and boots, she appeared shocked by the welcome and remained trapped inside her red BMW for several minutes. Two burly minders eventually forced a path through the surging pressmen and escorted her into the building. After giving her evidence, she was driven straight back to Heathrow airport to catch another Concorde flight. Because of work commitments she had been given only one day off.

Helen Danso, the 17-year-old from Bethnal Green, East London, who had threatened Liz with the knife, admitted the robbery. But her three accomplices pleaded not guilty. They were named as Christina Guerrine, who was 18 and also from Bethnal Green, Carlene Irving, an 18-year-old from Shepherd's Bush, and 17-year-old Tamara Flowers of Stratford, East London. However, after the three-day trial it took the jury less than an hour to find them all guilty. Remanding them in custody pending sentencing, Judge Gerald Butler, QC, warned them that they faced jail sentences.

Outside the court, the girls' families complained that they would have been treated differently in a lower profile case. 'They only got convicted because it was Liz Hurley,' said a woman claiming to be a friend of Carlene Irving. The girls were subsequently sentenced to 12 months in prison. The judge told them that the robbery was 'of a thoroughly nasty kind', but said he was satisfied they had shown 'genuine remorse'.

The trial had been brought forward to ensure that Liz could be with Hugh Grant in Hollywood for the Academy Awards ceremony the following week. But as she accompanied him on the big night, she was brought crashing down to earth by an unwitting snub from US chat show host Joan Rivers. 'Who are you?' Rivers asked a mortified Elizabeth on live television. 'This is Elizabeth Hurley, the new Estée Lauder girl,' Hugh gallantly explained, but Rivers, looking none the wiser, simply moved on to the next person. It was a painful reminder to Elizabeth that her four-and-a-half years in Hollywood had so far failed to make her a household name.

In the event, neither Hugh nor *Four Weddings* picked up any Oscars, although he had the honour of co-presenting the ceremony. At the post-Oscars *Vanity Fair* party, held at Mortons, it was clear to everyone that he was now a major player on the Hollywood scene. With Elizabeth by his side, wearing the kind of plunging white dress that had become a firm favourite, he rubbed shoulders with Hollywood's elite.

Thanks to her new Estée Lauder contract, Liz was leading a true jet-set lifestyle, flitting back and forth between London, New York and Los Angeles in first class. In April she was back in London for the British Academy of Film and Television Arts awards evening, where *Four Weddings and a Funeral* collected five BAFTAs and Hugh picked up the Peter Sellers Award for Comedy. But once again it was Liz who stole the evening, this time by wearing a fabulous pink flamenco-style dress loaned to her by the fashion designer John Galliano. There was no room for a bra, a fact that did not go unnoticed amongst the men in the room. 'That was very pleasant, I must say,' said the show's compere Billy Connolly after meeting her. 'Jiggling should be an Olympic event.' But the *Daily Mirror* nominated her as a prime candidate for a 'biffing' for 'allowing her breasts to give a one-woman VE Day tribute to the Dambusters'.

Chapter 5

In mid-May, she was once again draped on Hugh's arm for the US première of his film *The Englishman Who Went Up a Hill and Came Down a Mountain*. Her constant attendance at his side, coupled with her face appearing on Estée Lauder billboards, meant that the American public was starting to take notice of her in her own right. That same month she was placed fourth in the US magazine *People Weekly*'s annual round-up of the 50 most beautiful people in the world. She told the magazine how she and Hugh stood in front of the mirror 'deciding, if we have a baby, whose features it should have'. 'Her beauty is horribly marred by her ears,' Hugh chipped in, ungallantly. 'She looks like the F.A. Cup.'

However, all the adulation she was receiving for being the attractive arm candy of Hugh Grant could not hide the fact that her acting career was in the doldrums. Like *Beyond Bedlam*, her next film, *Mad Dogs and Englishmen*, also bombed. The movie, in which she played an upper-class heroin addict, was dismissed as 'hysterically over-written nonsense' by one reviewer, and her performance slated for generating 'the kind of excitement you get watching paint dry'. The *Observer*'s critic Lizzie Francke said Elizabeth had proved 'that she shouldn't give up all those days jobs'. She pronounced the movie 'a film to just say no to'. Liz was naturally hurt by the criticism but put it down to tall poppy syndrome, choosing to believe that the British Press wanted to knock her down to size because she was enjoying such success as a model.

The Englishman Who Went up a Hill and Came Down a Mountain was set to open in London in July 1995, but it was to be one première that Elizabeth would be in no hurry to attend. Hugh

That Dress

Grant, the man who had the world at his feet, was about to risk blowing it all by forsaking the love of his gorgeous girlfriend for the dubious charms of a $60 hooker ...

6 A Divine Scandal

In tabloid newspaper parlance, a truly sensational story can be crudely but accurately defined by its 'Fuck me!' factor: a story so astonishing, so unbelievable, that the reader will exclaim out loud when they read it.

The news of Hugh Grant's arrest with a Hollywood hooker had 'fuck me' written all over it.

In June 1995, Hugh was in Los Angeles where his new film, the romantic comedy *Nine Months*, was about to open. He was there without Elizabeth as, in a reversal of their normal living arrangements, she was in London where she had an important launch of her own to attend: that of the new Estée Lauder fragrance, Pleasures. On the morning of Tuesday June 27, she began her day in the Kensington offices of their film company, no doubt assuming that with Los Angeles being eight hours behind, Hugh was probably fast asleep in bed. But, in fact, Britain's most famous heartthrob actor was up and about and trawling the seedy red-light district of Hollywood's Sunset Strip. The man who, to the envy of red-blooded men everywhere, had shared Liz Hurley's bed for the past eight years was looking to pick up a prostitute for sex.

Chapter 6

Grant's first mistake, apart from not having a glass of hot milk and an early night, was driving a brand-new, white BMW – a car too flashy and expensive to escape the attention of the police officers who routinely patrolled the area. As he drove along Sunset Boulevard, he passed beneath the huge 20th Century Fox billboards advertising the eagerly awaited *Nine Months*. It was Hugh's first big-budget Hollywood film and everyone had high hopes of it being a major box-office success. As the romantic lead, his picture was plastered all over the posters, making him one of the most recognizable faces in town. All of which made what he was about to do next all the more difficult to fathom.

The police were on to him almost the minute he entered their patch shortly before 1 a.m. Vice cops Terry Bennyworth and Ernest Caldera immediately clocked the car and intuitively marked its driver as a potential suspect. Their suspicions were confirmed when the BMW crawled alongside a known prostitute on the corner of Courtney and Sunset. Hugh did not stop straight away, but suddenly appeared to have a change of heart and doubled back and pulled alongside the hooker. Blissfully unaware that his every move was being watched by vice officers, Grant gestured to the woman to get in the car and then drove quickly to Hawthorn Avenue, a quiet residential street nearby. The prostitute's name was Estelle Marie Thompson, a 25-year-old black woman who went by the street name of Divine Brown.

The officers, who had waited a few minutes to allow an offence to get under way, then did a double take as they noticed the BMW's rear lights flashing repeatedly on and off. The hapless Hugh had inadvertently kept his foot on the brake and was pressing the pedal with increasing urgency. But instead of the eagerly anticipated moment of ecstasy, the next moment he found himself staring into the faces of Bennyworth and Caldera as they shone their powerful flashlights through the window. They, in turn, saw Britain's favourite leading man lounging in the driver's seat with his trousers unzipped, receiving oral sex from Miss Brown.

In that second, Hugh Grant's glittering career must have flashed before his very eyes. But ordering the pair out of the car, the officers at first failed to recognize him. He was wearing a LA Dodgers baseball cap, pulled low over his face, and averted the policemen's gaze. Asked how much he had paid the prostitute for her services he quietly replied, 'Sixty dollars,' before being handcuffed and put in the back of an unmarked police car. Divine Brown was also handcuffed and placed in the back of a separate car, a matter of sad routine for her as she had prior convictions for prostitution. But as she waited to be taken to the police station, she saw the arresting officers talking to their colleagues and gesturing excitedly towards Hugh. Once they had asked Hugh for his ID it didn't take Bennyworth and Caldera long to realize that they had arrested the Hugh Grant – the one whose face was on giant billboards the length of Sunset Boulevard.

If Hugh had any hopes at all of keeping his arrest a secret, he couldn't have had them for long. The news broke with breathtaking speed and within 33 minutes of his arrest, a fax was received in the London newsroom of *The Times* from the LA Police Department's Press Office, outlining details of the alleged offence: lewd conduct. Elizabeth did not hear the news until almost two hours later. Sitting at her desk in the offices of Simian Films at noon British time, 4 a.m.in Los Angeles, she received two of the most upsetting phone calls of her life. The first was from her agent, who delivered the bombshell, followed a few seconds later by a call from Hugh himself.

Elizabeth was later to admit that when she heard what Hugh had done she felt as if she had been shot. Having to listen to her boyfriend crying at the end of the phone, telling her how every-thing had been a huge mistake and how sorry he was, was simply too much for her to bear. She ran out of the office in shock, not knowing what to do or where to go. For the past eight years he had been the person she had looked to for help when things went wrong. Now that he was the problem she did not know whom to turn to. So many painful emotions ran through her mind that day. Apart from the shock and hurt of Hugh's betrayal, and the humiliation that her boyfriend had chosen to pay for sex with a common prostitute, there was the embarrass-ment of his arrest and the uncomfortable publicity it would inevitably generate. They had been the golden couple of celebri-tydom, fêted for their film-star looks and glamorous, jet-set lifestyle. Now they would be a laughing stock.

As the story broke on the radio and television news, Britain gasped a collective 'Fuck me!' when it heard what its most famous actor had been up to. And as the rumour mill switched into overdrive, word went around that not only had Grant been caught with a prostitute; he had been caught with a transvestite prostitute. This particular rumour turned out to be incorrect, however. Divine Brown, as she was later to prove, was 100 per cent female.

The ever-helpful LAPD Press Office duly confirmed Grant's arrest to the world's journalists as they besieged its office with calls. Its Press release dryly detailed the particulars relating to suspect no. 4454813. 'Height 5-11; Hair Bro; Eyes Blu; Weight 175; Birthdate 09 09 60; Time arr 0115; Time bkd; 0229; Location of arrest 7560 Hawthorn Av ... charge and code 647 (A) PC ... Definition LEWD CONDUCT ... Bail $250'. Even more humiliatingly, the charge sheet details were accompanied by the full-colour police mug-shots of Hugh, who was pictured looking ashen-faced and downcast with his police suspect number printed below. The actor who always had a witty quip or throw-away remark for journalists, now looked for all the world like a deflated balloon. His picture was in stark contrast to Divine Brown's mug-shot, which showed her with her arms crossed in front of her and her head tilted back defiantly. Within a matter of hours, these pictures, together with the whole sorry story, would be plastered across the front pages of newspapers around the globe. Hugh Grant's down-fall had been nothing if not spectacular ...

After his tearful phone call to Elizabeth, which she terminated by hanging up on him, Hugh was released by the police. In view of his star status he was permitted to leave without having to find somebody to stand bail for him. He returned to the Four Seasons Hotel, where the cast of *Nine Months* was staying, to face his shocked co-stars and director. He then had to endure the unpleasant task of telephoning his parents in England to tell them the news. After the initial shock, James and Fynvola Grant were supportive of their youngest son. 'My father said, "Look here old boy, I've been in the army, I know about this sort of thing,"' Hugh later revealed.

Chapter 6

While Elizabeth and his parents were struggling to come to terms with the bombshell news, over at 20th Century Fox there was a mixture of disbelief and confusion. The company had spent an estimated $10 million dollars on a publicity campaign for *Nine Months*, only to face the very real prospect of having it all collapse around their ears. How could they promote Hugh as the whiter-than-white romantic hero when the whole world knew the seedy truth about him? The film could turn into one of the biggest flops on record if the notoriously conservative good people of Middle America refused to go and see it. With this in mind, within hours of Hugh's arrest the damage limitation exercise was in full swing. First, he made a humble statement of confession, which was hastily issued by his publicists. 'Last night I did something completely insane,' he said. 'I have hurt people I love and embarrassed people I work with. For both things I am more sorry than I can say."'

That day's scheduled press conference to promote *Nine Months* was cancelled and the waiting journalists informed that Hugh had a stomach ache that kept him confined to his room. A trailer for the film, which ironically showed Hugh's character in a police mug-shot, was hurriedly withdrawn from cinemas. A back-up advertising campaign had to be launched to replace the billboard posters of Hugh's co-star Julianne Moore whispering suggestively into his ear because they were attracting the unwanted attentions of witty graffiti artists.

The following day, Hugh fled Los Angeles for the sanctuary of his brother James's apartment in New York. This brought him a few hours' peace and quiet but on the other side of the Atlantic Elizabeth was not so lucky. She was swamped by journalists wanting to know what she thought about Hugh and the hooker, and her much-trumpeted launch as Estée Lauder's new cover girl looked like descending into farce. While Hugh's father had tried to be supportive of his son by taking the view that 'men will be men', Roy Hurley was livid with Hugh for treating his daughter so shabbily. 'He wanted to have him horse-whipped,' Elizabeth later admitted.

Unwilling to stay in her flat because of the ever-growing crowd of reporters camped outside, Liz sought refuge at the west London home of her friend Henry Dent-Brocklehurst. The upper-class Brocklehurst, a step-cousin of Camilla Parker Bowles, was to be Elizabeth's arch-defender at this time, offering a shoulder to cry on and issuing occasional bulletins to the Press on her behalf. Elizabeth, he informed everyone, was 'bearing up well' but was 'terribly crushed'. He appeared confident that the couple's relationship would ultimately survive the scandal. 'I am sure they will cope adequately,' he said. 'Liz is calm and collected and very supportive of him. She is coping extremely well. As far as I know, there is no question of them splitting up.'

But while Hugh hid out in the Manhattan luxury of his banker brother's apartment and Elizabeth licked her wounds in the privacy of Dent-Brocklehurst's Holland Park home, Divine Brown was not so fortunate. Like a particularly rare wild animal, she was being hunted down by the Press and now had a bounty on her head. Like Hugh, she had been bailed to appear in court at a later date, but upon leaving the police station she had apparently disappeared. Dozens of journalists descended on Sunset Boulevard, each of them under pressure from their news desks to make sure they found Divine Brown. The LA correspondent of *The Sun* even nailed 'wanted' posters to palm trees, offering Brown $150,000 for her story. Quick to spot a chance to make a buck or two, some of the reporters were ripped off by pimps claiming to represent Divine, or by prostitutes pretending to know where she was staying. Handfuls of dollar bills were handed over in the faint hope that one of them might be telling the truth. But still Miss Brown remained elusive.

Realizing that he couldn't hide away for ever, by Thursday Hugh had left New York and taken the five-hour flight back to Los Angeles. No sooner had his plane touched down than he boarded a private jet to England where he had the unenviable task of facing Elizabeth's legendary fury. 'I am terrified of Elizabeth,' he had previously told movie magazine *Premiere*. 'She's a very, very frightening person. Her rage knows no equal.' Elizabeth had good reason to be livid with Hugh. Apart from the very personal hurt she felt at his betrayal, she was also furious with him for having been so stupid. She worried that he might have thrown away not only his own career but quite possibly hers as well. She had been chosen to be the face of Estée Lauder because of her image as a fresh-faced English rose whose elegant beauty would hopefully persuade millions of women to part with their hard-earned cash in the hope of looking like her. Having a boyfriend who trawled seedy red-light areas looking to pick up prostitutes did not sit well with this image – or with the image of herself that she had spent so long cultivating.

It was a very real fear of Elizabeth's that she would be dumped by Estée Lauder at that time. After all, she had only been with them for five minutes and it was a company that was known to value its reputation as purveyors of the romantic idyll.

Tawdry headlines in which it was connected – however loosely – to LA street hustlers was not Estée Lauder's definition of what constituted good PR. But Elizabeth was saved by the loyalty of its president, Leonard Lauder. Although Lauder was far from pleased by the news of Hugh's indiscretion, he felt sufficiently confident of Elizabeth's ability to ride the storm to stand by her. 'Her contract with Estée Lauder remains unchanged,' he said. 'We stand by any decision Elizabeth makes in her personal life and have not offered her any advice. And of course our campaign is going forward as planned. We are supportive of Elizabeth in every way. She is terrific. We are extremely pleased with the work she is doing for us.' But an unnamed source at the company was quoted in the Press as saying, 'It is generally felt here that it would be better if Liz kept her distance, at least publicly, from Hugh.'

Liz was also concerned for the future of her and Hugh's company in Hollywood and the day after his arrest she was on the phone to executives at Castle Rock to assure them that it was 'business as usual' for Simian Films. Opinion was divided over the question of whether Hugh's sleazy antics would wreck his career as an upper-class romantic lead. Michelle Guish, the casting director for *Four Weddings and a Funeral*, was quoted in *The Times* as saying that the film industry would take his indiscretion with a pinch of salt. 'I wouldn't think it would harm him in a million years,' she said. But fellow casting director Beth Charkham disagreed. 'The Americans like their actors squeaky clean,' she pointed out. 'People who have been offering him £5 million for a picture will think twice now because he is bad publicity.' Art Murphy of the *Hollywood*

Reporter said Grant did not have an image big enough that any mud might tarnish it.

A man who accurately forecast the outcome was the publicist Max Clifford. From day one he said the arrest could work to both Hugh's and Elizabeth's advantage, providing that they played their cards right. 'This offence happened in America where Liz Hurley is virtually an unknown,' he said shrewdly. 'Estée Lauder can exploit this for millions of pounds worth of publicity. They should split up and get back together in time for the première of his next film.'

By Thursday, the story was still very much front-page news and the question on everybody's lips was 'Why?' This was quickly followed by 'What on earth was he thinking of?' and 'What will Liz do?' It was all too much for people to fathom, including Liz's loudest champions, the tabloid Press. Why, the papers wanted to know, was Hugh Grant so stupid as to go out for a hamburger when he had prime steak at home? Virtually every heterosexual man in Britain would give his eye teeth to be able to share the lovely Lizzie's bed, whereas Hugh Grant, to pardon a pun, had risked blowing it all by cavorting with a two-bit hooker. White-van drivers all over the country shook their heads in disbelief as they poured over their copies of *The Sun* and the *Daily Mirror*.

As Hugh prepared to fly home to face the music, Elizabeth braved the London launch for the new Estée Lauder fragrance Pleasures, a name which now appeared to have rather unfortunate connotations. The same day, she released a statement in which she announced to the world, in the dramatic style reminiscent of Diana, Princess of Wales, that she was 'very much alone'. 'I am still bewildered and saddened by recent events and have not been in a fit state to make any decisions about the future,' she said. 'For years I have turned to Hugh for help in difficult times and so now, even though my family and friends have been very kind, I am very much alone.'

Privately, Elizabeth was also extremely angry. She had remarked back in 1991 that 'When you really like someone as we do, neither of us should shame the other. That would be too much.' Now Hugh had gone and done just that and Elizabeth was in no mood to forgive. Worryingly for him, she had also said that if he ever had an affair she would shoot him. Her awesome temper was later evidenced by police when, a month after Hugh's arrest, the couple's London flat was burgled while they were in America. The police discovered a dent in the bathroom door, which they said matched exactly the shape of Hugh's BAFTA award for *Four Weddings and a Funeral*. The award lay in pieces on the floor, alongside a letter from Hugh, which had been angrily shredded.

Although Hugh would be arriving in London within a few hours, Liz left the capital and fled to their £900,000 rented farmhouse in the tiny hamlet of West Littleton, near Bath. She was followed down the M4 by an unshakeable cortège of vehicles containing members of the Press and, in the early hours of Friday morning, by Hugh himself. If Hugh had hoped to have his awkward showdown with Liz in private, he was to be sadly disappointed. By the time that his black Mercedes pulled into the drive at 1.15 a.m., the house was completely surrounded by reporters and photographers. The fact that it was the middle of the night made no odds – Fleet Street prides itself on never sleeping during a major news story.

Chapter 6

The following day saw the couple eating a tense lunch in the garden, their every movement captured by the dozens of long lenses that were pointing over the garden wall. The resulting photographs showed Elizabeth, flashing her legs in a tiny white tennis skirt and top and standing with her hands on her hips opposite a suitably cowed-looking Hugh. Things were clearly not going well for him. Events were beginning to resemble a rather badly produced play, with the Press as the audience and Hugh and Liz as leading man and lady. The couple could, after all, have taken their lunch indoors away from the cameras' prying eyes. But what happened next was to reduce it to pure pantomime.

As the newsmen and -women waited in the sweltering summer heat, a large van pulled up outside the farmhouse carrying a king-sized divan bed. The journalists could scarcely believe their luck. There, as bold as brass, was the proof that Hugh was being elbowed to the spare room! The bed company later confirmed the basic facts: the mattress had been ordered by Elizabeth on the day of Hugh's arrest, and was, she specifically told them, for the spare room. As Elizabeth walked her pet dog Nico around the country lanes later that afternoon, the contrast between her and Divine Brown could not have been more pointed. Dressed in jeans and wearing a simple short-sleeved checked shirt, she looked every inch the girl next door. It was an image that she had taken pains to convey. 'I think that Elizabeth uses the language of clothes very cleverly,' says Jane Proctor. 'When she's in a situation where she feels threatened she will retreat to jeans and a casual shirt which says, "I'm very wholesome."'

After spending 36 emotional hours with Hugh, it was apparent that Liz was not going to let him off lightly. The couple's raised voices could be clearly heard by the assembled Press pack and the next morning, in a move that signalled to the world that she could not face another day in the same house as Hugh, Elizabeth packed her bags and was driven away in a chauffeur-driven car. She had chosen her exit outfit equally carefully and left the house wearing a demure cotton frock studded with plastic ladybirds. Once again her destination was the home of her film producer pal Henry Dent-Brocklehurst, but this time she was heading to the sanctuary of his castle in Gloucestershire. Cocooned within the walls of his family home, Sudeley Castle, Elizabeth was at last safe from the prying long lenses of the media. With 60 staff to cater to her every whim, she took her mind off her troubles by reading old Enid Blyton books, immersing herself in the comforting stories of her childhood.

Fleeing into the arms of another man led to inevitable speculation that Liz was having a romance with Henry. He was known to lavish money on her in Los Angeles and she frequently played hostess during dinner parties at his Hollywood home. But although he admitted 'I adore her and we are close', he denied that there had ever been a romance between them. However, the situation was not helped by Brocklehurst's indiscreet revelations about his role in Elizabeth's life. 'Liz often stays at my house in LA even when Hugh is in town,' he said in an interview before Hugh's sex scandal erupted. 'Liz leads two lives and when she's not with Hugh she's here in LA with me.' Needless to say, it was not a set-up that Hugh felt happy about – especially given Brocklehurst's dismissive remark of him, in which he labelled

Hugh a 'bimbo boyfriend'. Liz's friendship with Brocklehurst had led to rows between her and Hugh on more than one occasion and Brocklehurst cheerfully recounted to the Press how Hugh had blown his top after he had taken Elizabeth on a pheasant shoot. 'We represent another world to Hugh,' he said, appearing to include Elizabeth in his 'we'. 'I know Hugh did not approve of the pheasant shooting. They had a bit of a row about that.'

While Liz was hidden away with her friend at Sudeley, Hugh was left with only Nico and a housekeeper for company. Photographed taking the dog for a walk, he cut a lonely, dejected figure.

If Liz had kept a low profile at Sudeley Castle, doubtless more people would have had more sympathy for her. But her next actions were to serve effectively to kill any feelings of empathy that people might have had for her and to plant the seed in some people's minds that she was actually enjoying all the attention. For within half an hour of arriving at Sudeley she had changed out of the ladybird dress and emerged wearing an eye-catching platinum blonde wig and bright pink jeans. It would be hard to imagine a get-up less likely to render a person invisible and the handful of journalists who had been staking out the estate were not fooled for a minute as to the mystery blonde's identity.

Brocklehurst then took her for a 45-minute spin in his open-top Porsche Carrera through the castle's grounds. Liz was seen laughing and joking, her shoulder-length wig cascading in the breeze. Her host tried to insist to reporters that the platinum blonde was a friend called Lucy Curry but on Sunday he appeared at the gates to issue a more sensible bulletin to the assembled throng. 'Liz will be leaving in the morning,' he announced grandly. 'She's probably leaving the country.' Asked how she was feeling, he replied that she was under a lot of stress and pressure but was 'certainly bearing up'. 'More than anything she just needs time to think about her relationship,' he said. 'She has made no decision. She is thinking over her future.'

Despite her high jinks with the dressing-up box, it was a difficult time for Elizabeth. Like the rest of the country, she had spent Sunday reading Divine Brown's version of events. For while she had been playing cat and mouse with the Press in Britain, Divine Brown had been leading reporters an equally merry dance in America. It transpired that she had not been in hiding after all, but had been with the *News of the World* all along. The paper couldn't resist crowing about its scoop and issued a triumphant bulletin on the Saturday night. 'There has been enormous world-wide speculation as to where Miss Brown has been since her encounter with Mr Grant and the police on Monday night,' it said. 'To save our rival newspapers further unnecessary expense in their fruitless and frustrating search for Miss Brown, we can confirm that she has been with journalists from the *News of the World* since Tuesday morning at a secret location. Miss Brown has provided a full and detailed account of what happened between her and Mr Grant.'

Divine, who had been paid a reported £100,000 for her exclusive story, even posed in a scarlet version of Elizabeth's famous safety-pin dress. Over several pages she described how Grant had told her she was 'gorgeous' and said it was his fantasy to have sex with a black woman. She claimed he had called himself Lewis and when she told him her name was Divine he had replied, 'You certainly are.' He was then said to have kissed her neck and told her that she smelt nice. When the paper had said that Miss Brown had provided them with a 'full and detailed account' of what had gone on between her and Grant, they meant it. No detail was spared as Divine divulged how her client had initially demurred at wearing a condom (mint flavoured), and had been rougher than she liked. But perhaps the most astonishing revelation of all was that Grant's apparent parsimony had led to his downfall. One of the film world's top earners – a man who commanded fees of up to $7 million a movie – could only produce three, rather crumpled $20 bills. 'If he had paid $40 dollars more we could have gone to a hotel,' Brown explained.

Henry Brocklehurst confirmed that Elizabeth had read the article, a sordid and lurid account which had made her stomach churn. 'She was upset but realistically she was expecting this sort of thing to come out,' he said. Hugh too had read the story and had telephoned Elizabeth at Sudeley to apologize once again. 'She needs some breathing space,' said Brocklehurst. 'She is obviously deeply upset about everything but I think time and space will allow it to blow over. She will pick up the pieces in a week or so but whether she will continue with her friendship and relationship with Hugh has yet to be decided.' This was in stark contrast to his comments earlier in the week, when he had appeared confident that the couple's relationship would survive. Asked to describe Liz's meeting with Hugh at the farmhouse the previous Friday, he replied, 'I think it was fairly frosty.'

Elizabeth's mother, speaking from her home in Hampshire on the Monday, confirmed that her daughter was 'deeply hurt and down' after reading the sleazy revelations. 'Liz rang me last night and she was not in particularly good spirits," said Angela Hurley. "She has spent a very difficult day, and things are certainly not easy. Liz said the house was under siege and admitted feeling very down.'

The reason Elizabeth was being pursued as much if not more than Hugh was because everyone wanted to know if she was prepared to forgive him. Her reaction was deemed to be crucial in determining whether the public – the people who paid to see his films – would be lenient with him. Hugh's arrest had got people wondering about the true nature of their relationship and even before the Divine Brown incident, Hugh had intimated that the romance was long gone. 'Liz stopped fancying me years ago,' he said in an interview earlier that year. 'She encourages the myth now because I'm her product. She thinks the more time we are together the better it is for business.' All of which made Elizabeth every bit as interesting to the Press and public as her errant partner. Her games of hide and seek served merely to focus more attention on her.

After leaving Sudeley Castle, she was chauffeur-driven back to West Littleton to see Hugh and pick up a change of clothes before heading to Paris, where she had a modelling assignment for Estée Lauder. As she left the farmhouse after spending three-and-a-half hours with her partner, she looked a picture of misery. But not everyone was convinced that her heartbreak was genuine. 'She had no need to declare publicly how bewildered, saddened and alone she felt,' said the *Daily Mail*. 'It was written all over her – in her unsmiling mouth, her hunched shoulders, her pallid face, her sunglasses in hand so that her reddened eyes could be appreciated properly. As she walked towards her silver Mercedes, she stared straight ahead and uttered not a word, seating herself alone on the back seat. Nobody had the temerity to applaud, but there was little doubt that Liz was giving the finest performance of her life ... As she gazed into the middle-distance, a forlorn, winsome look on her down-turned face, she was the incarnation of deserted, hard-done-by womanhood.'

Warming to its theme, the article continued, 'Liz is merely the latest wronged woman to have discovered that a saintly expression is the secret ace up every female sleeve. Princess Diana turned it into an art form.' There had already been scepticism about the true motive behind some of Liz's actions. 'There was the ridiculous theatre of the bed delivery in which Elizabeth was trying to telegraph to the world that they would be sleeping in separate beds for the time being,' said Toby Young. 'It was just a complete charade.'

But events were starting to turn in her favour. With the exception of her ill-fated decision to wear the blonde wig and pink jeans, the bulk of the photographs that appeared in the media showed a woman crushed and hurt by her boyfriend's betrayal. As a result, she gained the public sympathy that had previously eluded her. She was no longer 'Liz Hurley, shameless scene-stealer', she had become an innocent woman wronged by her beastly boyfriend. Crucially, it had also brought her to the attention of the American public. 'The best thing that ever happened to her was Hugh Grant's scandal,' says Hollywood reporter Marc Freden. 'Everybody started to look at her and asked, "Who's the girl that this clown would turn his back on?"'

On July 10, Hugh Grant also won himself some much-needed

public sympathy when he took the unprecedented step of going on American national television to explain his actions. The interview on Jay Leno's *Tonight Show* had been prebooked so he could promote *Nine Months* but when the Divine Brown incident blew up many people expected him to cancel. When the news broke that he was going to go on after all, the world's Press descended on the NBC studios at Burbank, California. Hundreds of sightseers drove through the night in the hope of catching a glimpse of show business's most talked-about actor, forcing Leno to go outside and laughingly implore the crowd, 'Go back to your homes!'

Whatever Grant's motives for agreeing to go on *The Tonight Show*, it must have taken a great deal of courage to walk out on stage that day. Former stand-up comedian Leno made his viewers wait a full half-hour before he finally brought him on. But no sooner had Hugh ambled on stage than his host hit him with the question on everyone's lips. 'What the hell were you thinking of?' he asked. 'Um, well, it's, er, it's, er, it's not easy,' stumbled Hugh. 'The thing is, people keep giving me tons of ideas on this one. I keep reading new psychological theories – I was under pressure, over-tired, or I was lonely, or I fell down the stairs when I was a child or whatever. That would be bollocks to hide behind that. I think you know in life pretty much what's a good thing to do and what's a bad thing and I did a bad thing. There you have it.'

The audience, immediately disarmed by the famous Grant charm, applauded warmly. The second question everybody wanted to know the answer to was 'What does your girlfriend think of it all?' 'She's been amazing about it … she's been very supportive and we're going to try to work it out,' said Hugh.

Cue more applause. The interview was a resounding success for Jay Leno, drawing a record 18.5 million viewers to the show, and was also considered to have done much to improve Hugh's standing in America. But not everyone was convinced by his performance. 'Star's sorrow: Was it just an act?' asked the *New York Post*. According to the paper's poll, many of its readers thought that it was.

The following day, June 11, Hugh's case was heard at Los Angeles Municipal Court. The offence of lewd conduct in a public place carried a maximum of six months' jail and a $1,000 fine, but Grant was to escape a prison term. He hired top Hollywood showbiz lawyer Howard Weitzman to represent him and chose not to appear in court in person. Weitzman pleaded 'no contest' to the charge on his behalf and Hugh was ordered to pay court costs and fines amounting to $1,180. He was also placed on two years' unsupervised probation and given two months to prove to the court that he had undergone AIDS counselling. To his eternal relief, he was told that, provided he stuck to the terms of the sentence, he would keep a clean record.

When she appeared in court two months later, Divine Brown was not so lucky. True, she had her £100,000 from the *News of the World* to console her – beside which her $1,350 fine appeared paltry – but she was also landed with six months in jail. It transpired that the mother of three had two previous convictions for prostitution and by continuing to solicit had violated the terms of her parole. Her lawyer gamely tried to persuade the judge that she had 'turned her life around' since June 27 and had been busy doing charity work, but the judge was not convinced. Divine Brown's life had indeed turned around since Hugh

Grant's arrest, but not in the way that her lawyer was claiming. Propelled to mini-stardom, she had been inundated with offers to promote sexy lingerie and had recorded a trailer for the radio station Hugh had been tuned into on the night of their tryst. She subsequently starred in a porn movie and moved to Las Vegas where she continued to live off her exploits as the hooker who shamed Hugh Grant.

To many people's surprise, Elizabeth attended the US première of *Nine Months* with Hugh that evening. With his sentence out of the way, he looked happy and relaxed but she looked for all the world as if she wished she wasn't there. In contrast to her usual appearances at premières, where she generally wore plunging necklines and a knockout smile, she looked stony-faced and aloof. Refusing to crack a smile for anybody, she wore a short white dress with an unusually demure neckline and a simple gold crucifix around her neck. As usual, she had chosen her outfit with the utmost care and consideration for the message she wanted to impart. Yet again she was letting her clothes do the talking and yet again it was an unqualified success. 'She got across the message that she was utterly beautiful and made everybody wonder what on earth Hugh was thinking of,' explains Jane Proctor.

Over the years Liz has learned never to underestimate the power of white. 'When you monitor the clothes she's worn at key moments in her career, the white dress seems to be a favourite she comes back to,' says *The Times*'s film critic Sean Macaulay. 'It's always the white dress and there's something quite funny about that body being cloaked in virginal white. It creates a certain erotic tension which is very effective.'

Like everyone else, Liz's former flatmate Birgit Cunningham had been inordinately shocked when she heard the news of Hugh's arrest. 'I wasn't living with Liz at that time but when I heard the news my legs buckled,' she says. 'I couldn't believe it. But Liz is always good in a crisis and she handled the whole thing really well. I remember at the première everyone was looking to see how she would cope with being Hugh's girl-friend, and she just did it so perfectly, turning up in the white dress and crucifix and standing by her man. America is very puritanical so I think she got a lot of respect for that. It worked very well in her favour. That's when she definitely became famous in the States.'

Elizabeth now had the support and sympathy of the American public as well as the folks back home. Overnight she had gone from being an actress who was sneered at for her lack of talent and derided for being merely an accessory on Hugh Grant's arm to being perceived as a dignified and loyal woman of substance. *Nine Months* also benefited from the interest gener-ated by the Divine Brown incident. From the minute it opened on July 12 it was clear to the film company that they had a huge box-office success on their hands. People turned out in their droves, all anxious to catch a glimpse of the scandal-stricken star. Its director, Christopher Columbus, admitted that the film was receiving more attention because of Grant's troubles. 'I'm not egotistical enough to think the movie would be this big without it,' he said.

The day after the première, Hugh once again appeared on national television to bear his soul to the American public. This time he was interviewed by CNN's tough-talking chat-show host Larry King – a man who, in contrast to the amiable Jay Leno, was not prepared to let a difficult question go unanswered. Over and over again he asked Hugh, 'Why? Why did you do it? What made you do it?' But each time Hugh deftly sidestepped the question. Hugh also went on CBS's live *Late Show with David Letterman* but despite all his television appearances and the acres of newsprint spawned by his arrest, people would never really know why he had done what he did. A throw-away remark that he made during an interview in February 1994 goes some way to providing an explanation. 'My problem is that I have always found strangers sexy,' he said. 'If I do sex scenes early on with an actress, it is sexy. If I do it near the end of making a film and I know someone really well, then it tends to be a professional thing.'

Hugh's biographer Jody Tresidder has an interesting theory about it all. She believes that Hugh was actually living out a scene from the Martin Amis novel, *Money*. In the 1984 bestseller, the anti-hero, who is also in the film business, drives down Sunset Boulevard and picks up a hooker on impulse. The incident concludes with the man lying in the front seat of his car with his trousers round his knees, 'copping a $20 blowjob'. 'Was it possible that Hugh Grant, who sometimes complained to journalists that he wasn't sure who he was, couldn't even cheat on Elizabeth without a script?' Tresidder pondered.

By the middle of July, the strain appeared to be telling on Elizabeth. Flying back to London and leaving Hugh in Los Angeles, she lost her cool when newsmen asked her why he was not with her. 'Why do you ask such irritating questions?'

she snapped. 'I've come back to work and Hugh is in America working too.' Asked if their relationship was still on, she replied, 'I don't think you should ask questions like that. I wouldn't ask you if your wife had done something bad.' But never one to pass up an opportunity for self-promotion, no matter how it had arisen, she grabbed the chance to go on national US television. After five-and-a-half years of living in Los Angeles she was still unknown to the American public – until her boyfriend's moment of madness with a streetwalker had made her a star. Like Hugh, she found herself inundated with requests to appear on some of the biggest TV shows in the country but, in a decision which would effectively serve once again to upstage him, she said yes to only one of them – America's queen of celebrity interviewers, Barbara Walters.

Liz flew to New York on July 26 to record the interview for Walters's ABC news magazine show, *20/20*. It was taped in the suite of a Manhattan hotel, with Elizabeth dressed in an orange sweater paired with her trade-mark skin-tight black trousers. She had chosen her outfit carefully, with her fluffy jumper lending a girl-next-door touch to her perfectly groomed appearance. She had also chosen her interviewer carefully as Barbara Walters was well known for treating her celebrity guests with kid gloves. Sure enough, Walters began the interview by cosily asking Liz about her job as the new Estée Lauder model and enquiring about her upcoming film, *The Spear*. When Walters gently broached the subject of Hugh, asking if it had been love at first sight, Elizabeth's reply couldn't have been less romantic. She explained how they had been astounded by their similarities – how much alike they looked, how both their fathers were

retired army officers and their mothers schoolteachers special-
izing in the piano. 'So is that what attracted you – the two of you
had similar backgrounds?' asked Walters, clearly surprised by
Elizabeth's detached account of their relationship. 'Was it a
romance? Is it a romance?'

Elizabeth's answer did nothing to dispel the rumours that she
and Hugh had become more like brother and sister than lovers.
'I sort of feel he's my family,' she said. 'I think blood is very thick
… you're very at home with each other.' Moving on to the never-
to-be-answered question of why Hugh had gone with a hooker,
Walters asked Elizabeth if she knew why. 'Well, I think that most
things in life you do because you want to,' she said sharply. 'I
always think that to be the bottom line. There's all sorts of
psychobabble you can come up with. I think ultimately you
want to do something and you do it.'

Pushed finally into revealing what state her relationship with
Hugh was in at that moment, Liz admitted that she simply
didn't know. 'I'd like to say that everything's getting easier and
easier, falling into place, but it isn't really,' she said. 'I keep
saying to myself, what if instead the telephone call had been –
he's been killed in a car crash? That's 10 billion times worse.'
Walters, bizarrely seeming to suggest that that might have been
preferable, said, 'In a car crash he would be gone for ever and
there's no embarrassment, there's only sympathy and love left.'
'Yeah, but lost for the rest of my life,' Liz pointed out. Asked if
she would ever be able to understand or forgive Hugh's actions,
she replied, 'I don't think there's a question of understanding.
Forgiveness is a difficult subject. But that's something that has to
be worked out. It would be very easy now to become very hard.'

Elizabeth's interview, which was shown on August 4, was a triumph. It was the second most watched programme in the USA that week and was seen by some 20 million viewers. By the end of the week everyone in America was finally aware who Elizabeth Hurley was. But by the time it was aired, Liz had flown to South Africa to start work on *The Spear*, a film later renamed *Dangerous Ground*. At a press conference in Sun City to promote her role as a stripper in the movie, she admitted that she was looking forward to having a break from the British Press. But with true comic timing, she was then asked by a South African reporter if it was true that she would be posing for their edition of *Playboy* magazine while she was there. 'If that's what you have heard, I'm afraid you are very much misinformed,' said Liz sniffily.

She spent eight weeks filming her role as the girlfriend of a man embroiled in a drug cartel, co-starring with the American rap artist Ice Cube. As soon as the film wrapped at the end of September, she flew back to London for a reunion with Hugh. She was described as 'wreathed with smiles' as the pair went to a restaurant near their home, prompting the *Daily Mirror* to express its relief that Liz was 'no longer surly Hurley'. Proving the old adage that every cloud has a silver lining, her forgiveness of Hugh had catapulted them both into the super-league of celebrity couples on both sides of the Atlantic. 'Both Hugh and Elizabeth played it perfectly,' states Toby Young. 'They exploited the moment incredibly well and it was the making of her.'

That is also the opinion of the *News of the World*'s American editor, Stuart White. 'Before Divine Brown, nobody knew who the heck Liz Hurley was,' he said, speaking on the Channel 5 television documentary, *Liz Hurley's Brains*. 'I think she instinctively understood that now was not the time to jump ship. She had a good relationship with Hugh Grant and instinctively she stood by him. But at the back of her mind I can't help feeling that she was thinking, "This is not a bad career move either. If I just dump this guy I am just another wronged woman. But here I have all this sympathy." I think she is too clever not to have realized that that was a good thing for her.'

7 Liz Calls the Shots

As the hurt of Hugh's betrayal began slightly to ease, Elizabeth realized that some good had indeed come out of the whole sorry saga. Her triumphant appearance on Barbara Walters's show had raised her profile in America and she had emerged from the scandal smelling as sweetly as the Estée Lauder perfumes she promoted. Unlike many of her fellow Brits who went to Hollywood but failed to grasp what makes the town tick, Liz knew the importance of self-promotion and had a natural predilection for it. She had, after all, been doing it for years. What she had lacked thus far was a lucky break: something that would set her apart from all the other beautiful woman in Los Angeles and push her name into the limelight in the US. Hugh Grant's arrest, hurtful though it had undoubtedly been, had ironically been that break.

Both she and Hugh were now hot news in Hollywood and Liz instinctively moved to capitalize on their new status as one of the world's most talked-about celebrity couples. 'The thing about Elizabeth Hurley is that she's smart,' explains Hollywood reporter Marc Freden. 'Most stars don't understand that you have to be proactive in your own career. Agents and managers are facilitators to some extent, but if you don't have any marketability they are not going to push for you. If you go into any nightclub in this town you will see women who are as beautiful, or more beautiful, than Elizabeth Hurley. This town is full of beautiful people and she does not have the kind of rarefied beauty of Elizabeth Taylor, whose looks could guarantee her a lifetime of work. But the thing she has going for her is that she's a shameless self-promoter. People from England think that is gross. You have the tall poppy syndrome whereby you are not supposed to stand there and pat yourself on the back. But over here you get nowhere, and I mean nowhere, unless you are a shameless self-promoter. It's all about marketing. You are selling a product, and the product for her is Elizabeth Hurley.'

As Hugh Grant candidly admitted, Liz considered him to be her product too and she was determined to sell them both. 'When Hugh became successful, people thought they could make money out of him,' she said. 'Sometimes you use those people to get something you want yourself. For example, if someone is being incredibly nice to me to get to Hugh, and they have something that I want, then I'll take it.' Liz now knew how to play things the American way. 'You have to be tenacious, you have to work hard, and you have to throw away a little of that English putting yourself down because it doesn't translate at all,' she said.

As far back as 1991, she had expressed a desire to get into film production and realized that now was her big chance. Simian Films pitched an idea to Castle Rock for a film starring Hugh, which she would produce. Although Hugh was a proven leading man, she had no experience at producing a movie but such was the couple's cachet at the time, Castle Rock immediately commissioned the project. The movie was *Extreme Measures*, a hospital thriller about a mad scientist who preys on helpless vagrants. Hugh and Liz were lucky enough to get the eminent Hollywood actor Gene Hackman to play the twisted scientist, with Hugh cast as the hero doctor who saves the day.

Elizabeth had learned a lot from the events that followed Hugh's arrest. Discovering how a potentially ruinous event could be turned into a public-relations success was an invaluable lesson and she understood how things worked in Hollywood far better. Her time in Los Angeles could now be neatly separated into two distinct periods: Before Divine Brown and After Divine Brown. 'The way she seized the opportunity showed that she understood the way LA worked a lot more,' says film critic Sean Macaulay. 'When she first came to Los Angeles in the early 1990s she had been part of the dissolute English set and hadn't taken it all that seriously, taking the view that things would either happen or not. But after the Hugh Grant incident she was much more systematic about wooing the important people in high positions.'

The notion of Elizabeth Hurley, Hollywood movie executive seemed strangely at odds with her better-known image of Liz Hurley, tabloid babe. But she had no plans to let her male fans down by becoming shy and retiring, a fact she demonstrated by appearing in a sexy photo shoot for *Esquire* magazine. She appeared on its front cover in a skin-tight leather catsuit and high-heeled shoes. The inside photographs were even raunchier. In one she was shown on all fours, wearing nothing but a black leather bra, studded thong, black patent leather boots and a blonde wig. In another provocative shot she wore white socks and a black see-through baby-doll nightie with stiletto-heeled shoes, clasping a teddy-bear to her chest. She told the magazine that she and Hugh were 'playing each day as it comes' but professed to now hating England. 'I can't stand being followed and watched,' she moaned.

According to her journalist friend William Cash, Liz was considering going to live in Ireland in order to escape the British Press – a story that she subsequently denied. In an article for the October 1997 edition of *Harpers & Queen* magazine, Cash said she was planning to settle in Ireland and convert to Catholicism. She was said to have been receiving instruction from Father Alexander Sherbrooke, a parish priest in Twickenham, Middlesex. But describing the claim as 'absolute baloney', a rather cross Father Sherbrooke denied giving her instruction. 'I have never met or spoken to Elizabeth Hurley,' he told the *Daily Mail*. 'I may have some old school friends who knew Hugh Grant but that's as close as my connection to Elizabeth is. The wish to become a Catholic comes from the soul. It's not a simple matter of saying "I fancy being Catholic" and that's it. The Catholic Church may seem quite glamorous with its custom and tradition, but being a Catholic is a serious matter. It is also an intensely private matter. People often receive instruction for many years. If Elizabeth Hurley were to bowl up this morning and say she wanted to become a Catholic, I would say we had to go for a very long talk.'

Given that a photograph of Liz shaking hands with the Pope had appeared in a newspaper that very week, the *Daily Mail* was not alone in considering that her motives might have more to do with 'worship at the altar of publicity' than genuine religious fervour. William Cash hastily tried to limit the damage. 'That's a monstrous suggestion,' he told the paper. 'She's almost obsessed with the Catholic faith. I think there has been a slight misunderstanding. If there has, it's the fault of the editors at the magazine or mine. It's certainly not Elizabeth's. She's not actually converting, she's just considering it.'

Elizabeth had met the Pope when she was filming *Dangerous Ground* in Pretoria. Her audience with the pontiff was arranged by Sun City hotelier Gerry Inzerillo, who revealed that Liz had commissioned a photographer to take pictures of them both. 'It was a very special moment for her,' he said. 'Elizabeth is very interested in theology and said she was about to convert to Catholicism. It was a private meeting but we'd discussed the possibility that the photographs might leak out.' However, some people were left wondering if Liz's interest in Catholicism was just another example of her infatuation with Evelyn Waugh. Catholicism features strongly in many of Waugh's books, most particularly in *Brideshead Revisited*, and the author had himself converted to the faith when he was twenty-seven. Rather peculiarly, Liz claimed to have had 'strange dreams' as a teenager. 'I longed to be stigmatic and, of course, I never was,' she said. 'But you go through that stage where you think you could be a nun and wouldn't it be marvellous if you started bleeding.'

As well as pursuing her acting career and trying her hand at film producing, Liz was also busy with her role as the Estée Lauder girl. It had taken her quite a while to adjust to her new career, which she entered at an age when most models retire. She also considered that she had been handed the lucrative modelling contract on a plate, something that did not sit easily with her. 'It is quite a weird feeling if you've really struggled for a long time to get somewhere in your chosen profession and then suddenly someone offers you something in a different profession, which is immediately at a higher stage than you've managed to achieve so far,' she explained in an interview with the *Observer*. 'In a way, it seems to belittle what you've done before because you don't feel as if you've deserved it or earned it. I'd never got anything for nothing in my life, but that was one thing that I did get absolutely for nothing.'

The Estée Lauder campaign featuring her face was being run in a hundred different countries worldwide and involved an enormous amount of travelling. Although the job of a supermodel may appear glamorous, Liz soon discovered that in reality it is extremely hard work. When she was in New York, where most of her modelling work took place, a typical day would see her starting work well before 8 a.m. A limousine would collect her from her luxury hotel in uptown Manhattan and deliver her to the West Village studios of Estée Lauder's photographer, Albert Watson, the man whom Elizabeth credits with teaching her how to pose.

After a long morning's shoot, they would break for lunch at one, but Watson's models never go out to eat. Instead, low-calorie fare is provided, such as carrot soup, tuna pitta bread, grilled vegetables and fresh fruit. Liz may have claimed on the David Letterman show to eat 'like a pig', but, having watched her weight since she was a teenager, she was now under more pressure than ever to be thin. For someone who once admitted that she couldn't follow a low-fat diet because it makes her want to 'kill people', this was far from easy. Her favourite food is hearty, fattening dishes like liver and bacon with mashed potato, and ravioli stuffed with ricotta cheese, but she could now allow herself such treats only rarely. 'She was definitely never fat but she dropped so much weight once she got the Estée Lauder contract,' remarks her former flatmate Birgit Cunningham.

After lunch, Liz would go back into make-up and then spend the rest of the afternoon being photographed. The shoot would not usually finish until 6 p.m., by which time she would have notched up a ten-hour day. If the shoot was carrying on the following day there would be no wild nights out on the town for her either. Instead, it would be a light dinner and an early night, preferably with nothing more exciting than a good book. 'I have hardly any treats,' she said mournfully in an interview with *The Sunday Telegraph*. 'I can't go to bed late, can't eat too much.' The only vice she allowed herself was her beloved cigarettes, which had the added advantage of suppressing hunger pangs.

Apart from smoking – which most models do despite the fact that it causes unsightly lines around the mouth – Liz approached her modelling contract with the utmost dedication. 'Elizabeth is very professional and always rests in the evening so she looks her best the following day,' says Albert Watson's wife, Elizabeth. On days where she had other obligations, such as television interviews, Liz would have to get up even earlier to squeeze them in before she started work. She also had to make time to work out in the gym – something she hated immensely as she had always disliked exercise.

Liz naturally got a thrill out of seeing her face on giant bill-boards and the front covers of glossy magazines, and was universally admired for her English rose beauty. But her acting work was still failing to set the screen alight. In May 1996, *Dangerous Ground* was released on an unsuspecting public, featuring Liz – complete with dodgy Afrikaner accent – playing a drug addict stripper with an AK-47 rifle. 'I would really love this film to be a success and for people to like it and learn something from the film,' she said, somewhat optimistically. But people didn't like it and it bombed badly at the box office. However, in August 1996 she landed the role that was to be her most successful to date. Mike Myers, the American star of the hit movie *Wayne's World*, was to play a James Bond-style playboy in the espionage spoof, *Austin Powers: International Man of Mystery*. Liz, in an inspired piece of casting, was hired to play his prim assistant Vanessa Kensington.

As a model, she was under a great deal of pressure not simply to be thin, but to look as perfect as she possibly could. She needed to have a flawless complexion, glossy hair, perfectly manicured nails, and a body that was waxed, buffed and polished to perfection. The combination of her natural good looks and Estée Lauder's extensive team of manicurists, make-up artists and stylists meant that this was not too difficult to achieve. But in one area at least she definitely appeared to have gone a step further. At the US première of *Extreme Measures* in September 1996, she showed off unusually plump, bee-stung lips, prompting speculation that she had had collagen injections. Her spokesman denied it, saying that her new look was down to 'lip pencil and gloss' but there was a definite change in her mouth. One wag even commented that it now resembled that of the full-lipped Divine Brown.

'Someone has pumped Liz's lovely mouth full of collagen, creating strange lines around the edges,' commented *The Guardian*'s Emma Forrest. 'When she smiles, she looks in pain.' Forrest said that she didn't like the new thin, wan Liz at all, and it was true that Liz was starting to look most unlike her old voluptuous self. Her recognizable glossy dark brown hair was gone, replaced by an unflattering shade of blonde, and the famous Hurley curves were also fast disappearing. In the ads to promote Pleasures, Estée Lauder had her wandering through a field of flowers in a style reminiscent of the actress Jane Seymour's campaign for Le Jardin perfume. But while Miss Seymour successfully built an entire career on her image as the quintessential English rose, that approach did not somehow seem quite right for the sex bomb who had wowed Britain in the Versace safety-pin dress.

'The cosmetics giant has been erasing Hurley and everything that she stood for,' Forrest complained in her article. 'She did possess a tough, urban, post-industrial beauty. What did Estée Lauder do? Make her pose in a field of pink flowers, surrounded by puppies. You can be an English rose and still have thorns. Liz surrounded by puppies is so embarrassing, so wrong. With each new ad she is getting mousier, until one day we'll wake up and our English rose with thorns will have been turned into Carolyn Besette Kennedy or any of those skinny, bland blondes. She was our tabloid goddess and everything was big – her eyes, mouth, breasts, hair, eyebrows – she was like five sex symbols for the price of one.'

Like many people, Forrest had been shocked at how unbelievably skinny Elizabeth appeared in the Austin Powers film.

'Seeing her wear a PVC catsuit, your first thought is, "Why isn't she seeing a doctor?"' she said. 'This person cannot be well. Hurley is too thin for her own body.' Forrest lay the blame squarely at the doors of Estée Lauder. 'It knew what it was getting – a curvy, sexy woman who slept in her make-up and swore she never exercised,' she wrote. 'Everyone knows that multi-million dollar ad campaigns involve a little airbrushing. But this one is not so much airbrushing a great British sex symbol as Tippexing her out altogether.'

Elizabeth was later to reveal that she had made herself ill by not looking after herself correctly. 'I got very ill, very thin, and ruined my digestion by not eating properly,' she told the *Mail on Sunday* in 1999. Although she was at pains to point out that she didn't have an eating disorder, she admitted that when stressed she loses her appetite and gets 'terrible' stomach pains. Realizing that she had radically to change the way she handled pressure, she spent over a year learning to 'sit down, calm down, eat something like a boiled egg … otherwise I'd end up in hospital', she said candidly. By 1997, Elizabeth had lost so much weight and was working so hard that her friends were worried about her. She was regularly working seven days a week, leaving no time for holidays. 'I'm at that stage where I want to work as hard as I can,' she explained at the time. 'There is a certain amount of seizing the day because I have previously felt powerless to improve my position. I have always wanted to be successful. I don't think there's anything wrong with that.'

As well as dealing with pressure in her career, Liz had to face personal heartache when her father died suddenly during a trip to Paris with her mother in 1996. Roy Hurley was only 67 years old and his unexpected death left Liz shocked and deeply distraught. It is a tragedy that she has felt unable to speak about publicly. 'It made me realize that most of the things I worry about are unimportant,' she said in a rare reference to his death. The following July she faced further distress when her friend Gianni Versace was gunned down and killed outside his home in Miami. As if that was not shocking enough for Elizabeth, she later discovered that her name was apparently on a celebrity hit list found at the home of his assassin, Andrew Cunanan. It was her worst nightmare come true as ever since she had moved to America in the early 1990s, she had worried about becoming the victim of a crazed stalker. It was why she had learned to shoot and she had even gone as far as to chose which gun she would buy. But in the end she decided that owning a gun was an even scarier proposition and contented herself with getting a dog for protection. The shock news of Versace's apparently motiveless murder served to magnify her already paranoid fear of stalkers. Just days before his death she had been photographed sunbathing at the house she and Hugh were renting on Cherokee Drive in Los Angeles. 'What if,' she couldn't help thinking, 'that paparazzo had been an assassin?'

As the producer of *Extreme Measures*, Elizabeth enjoyed issuing instructions to the cast and crew, including Hugh – whom she made address her as Miss Hurley on set. 'We've always taken our work home with us anyway, so this was putting an official stamp on what we had unofficially been doing for years,' she explained. 'It was cool. I think it was nice for Hugh to feel there was someone supporting him and looking out for him on set.' Being bossed around by Elizabeth was a situation that Hugh had been familiar with for years, but he found working with her to be infinitely more scary. 'She's always been a bossy control freak, so nothing's changed there,' he said. 'In this case, she just got paid for it. We all lived in fear of her. We fought about everything but Elizabeth always won.'

Liz readily admitted to being dominating. 'I was bossy as a child and I'm bossy still,' she said. 'I can't bear it when people do things I know I can do better. Then I find I can't do them better myself and I get very upset. Tolerance is not one of my great strengths. I don't like people who cross me. It's a question of standards. Mine are rather high.' She confessed to having berated a laid-back office girl for not running to the fax machine quickly enough when a fax came through, but said she had no idea how obsessed she would become with producing films. 'I was being so very, very hands on, not because of anything to do with my ego, but just because I couldn't bear for every aspect of it not to be the very, very best it possibly could be,' she said in a TV interview. 'I don't think I wanted to produce just for the sake of being in control. It was about having a vision and being in a position where you can try your hardest to make sure it's accomplished. It's a nice feeling but there were plenty of times when I was wrong and I was happy to admit "OK, forget it, you're right, let's do it your way".'

Liz's and Hugh's working relationship may have been full of sparks but rumours continued to circulate that their private life was not. Stories alleging Liz's affair with Tom Sizemore were published in the British and American Press and in April 1997 she appeared in the French scandal magazine *Paris-Match* with a 'mystery man'. The pictures showed her lying topless by the pool at her Beverly Hills home, having suntan oil rubbed into her bottom. Headlined 'Liz flaunts her revenge', the two-page article said the tables had been turned on the unfaithful Hugh, although Elizabeth later claimed the mystery man was her brother Michael.

Disappointingly for Elizabeth, *Extreme Measures* was not a success either at the box office – where it failed to recoup its costs – or for Hugh Grant. But she had managed to bring in the entire project more than a million dollars under budget, which is the kind of rare feat that gets a producer noticed in Hollywood. The film's director, Michael Apted, was also impressed with her production debut. Apted, who directed the acclaimed *Gorillas in the Mist*, admitted he had initially been sceptical, but had been won over by her enthusiasm. 'If she was unsure about something, she would ask,' he said in an interview. 'Elizabeth is a hands-on producer at all times. She was the one who had the passion for this project. She was determined to get it made.' For her part, Liz had thoroughly enjoyed making a film in America. 'I like the response here,' she said. 'If you say to someone, "I've got a great idea," and they think they can make money, they say, "Great, let's do it." It's as simple as that.'

May 1997 saw the unveiling of her latest foray into acting, playing the biblical seductress Delilah in the American TV mini-series, *Samson and Delilah*. But once again her performance was savaged by the critics. 'An excruciating dud' was one verdict, while others returned to the sorry story of Hugh's sex shame. 'Hurley, a sort of anaemic Jacqueline Bisset, preens and leers in a desperate attempt to seem sexy. Would we have heard of her if her boyfriend hadn't been caught with his pants down?'

wrote one. The ghost of Divine Brown lingered infuriatingly on. 'It still causes me pain,' Liz admitted to an American reporter. 'But I have thrown myself into work to block out the memories. You have to make a choice to sink or swim. I have a loyalty to people who have put trust and money in me, so I chose to swim. It didn't occur to me to collapse into a little heap and not capitalize on the run of good luck I was having. I had no choice but to carry on and go to work every day, and every evening too.' She pointed out that she was not the kind of person to run for cover. 'You can either hide under the dining room table or get on with things,' she said matter-of-factly. 'I'm not the type of woman who hides.'

Her portrayal of Delilah may have failed to impress, but when *Austin Powers: International Man of Mystery* opened in America Elizabeth experienced something completely new: a favourable review. The talent for comedy that her drama tutor had first noticed at the London Studios Centre had finally brought her critical acclaim. 'Elizabeth Hurley is easy on the eyes as Vanessa Kensington and shows a real flair for comedy,' praised the *New York Daily News*. The movie took $7.5 million in the US within days of opening, and made Elizabeth hot property as an actress. A single box-office success had served to render all her previous flops instantly forgotten and she secured roles in two major Hollywood films on the back of it.

She was offered a rumoured £3 million to appear in the romantic comedy *EDtv*, opposite Matthew McConaughey and Woody Harrelson, and was also signed up to appear with Christopher Lloyd and Jeff Daniels in the Walt Disney comedy spoof *My Favourite Martian*. *EDtv* was a somewhat ironic choice of film for Liz, given that it was about the media's obsession with celebrity and saw her cast as a scantily dressed model who hitches a ride on her boyfriend's fame. She admitted she had enjoyed filming scenes with heartthrob Matthew McConaughey, even though the two of them had had trouble with each other's accents. 'It was very nice,' she said. 'A lot of snogging with Matthew, a lot of rolling around. On a non-verbal level we got along really well.' But try as she may, she couldn't understand her co-star's Texan drawl, while her clipped English accent had him all at sea.

With the success of *Austin Powers* and a flurry of films in the pipeline, Liz was at long last being taken seriously in Hollywood. 'Hurley isn't the joke figure some people would like you to think she is,' a British producer in Los Angeles was quoted as saying. 'She works hard, really hard.' For her part, Liz considered that people's initial perceptions of her worked in her favour. 'I've always thought you're at a distinct disadvantage if anybody underestimates you,' she said shrewdly. 'You slide in and take people by surprise. The best part of fame is that I get to do parts that I wanted to do for so long. Before this success, I would sit around praying the phone would ring.'

Simian Films' next project was *Mickey Blue Eyes*, a comedy about the Mafia starring Hugh in the lead role and Jeanne Tripplehorn as his love interest. The veteran Hollywood hell-raiser James Caan was cast to play Tripplehorn's mobster father. Liz was responsible for everything from raising the money to make the film to hiring the director and developing the script. But despite the inherent problems involved in film-making, she was in her element. 'I've been sweating buckets,' she said. 'There is always something to do. I wake up in the middle of the night, worrying about the most minute details, like where the extras will park their cars. I actually like the panic, it has to be said. I like Pressure that is sort of relentless. I get a certain satisfaction out of that at the end of the day. It revs my energy.'

While filming *Mickey Blue Eyes* in New York in early 1998, she was under additional pressure because she was trying to quit smoking. She later claimed that it had been the most stressful period of her life. 'I was so angry the whole time, so I gave in and started smoking again,' she said. 'It was really pathetic. I started saying to myself, "I only have one nice thing in my life, and now I don't even have that."' She and Hugh also spent time talking to genuine New York mobsters in the interests of research, and Liz even gave some of their girlfriends roles as extras. James Caan claimed that when they were filming a scene in which he and Hugh had to bury a corpse in a New Jersey landfill, a childhood friend warned him, 'Don't dig too deep around here.'

In May 1998, Liz and Hugh had a wedding to attend but to the disappointment of the British Press, it was not their own. Henry Dent-Brocklehurst finally put paid to the rumours about him and Liz by marrying somebody else. He and Hawaiian model Lili Maltese tied the knot in the private chapel at Sudeley Castle. But Liz, in one of her most shameless acts of scene-stealing yet, appeared determined to outshine the bride. She turned up to the evening reception wearing a bright scarlet dress, slashed almost to the waist and displaying her leopardskin print knickers for all to see. The dress was another Versace creation and had been designed especially for her by Gianni's sister, Donatella. If anything, it even eclipsed the famous safety-pin dress, prompting one commentator to label it 'Indecent exposure on legs'. Liz had successfully managed to make herself the centre of attention once again, but this time the stunt threatened to back-fire. To have worn such a dress to a première would have been one thing, reasoned her detractors; to wear it to a wedding was quite another. Liz came in for bucketloads of criticism – mainly from women writers – who considered that this time she had gone too far.

'Surely, this must be the end of a friendship,' said Brenda Polan, writing in the *Daily Mail*. 'Consider the position of Lili Maltese. On her wedding day she is completely upstaged by the woman she thought of as a friend. Among people with taste and discretion … it is hard to imagine anything more tasteless, unless it is the dress itself. [It] would have been quite at home on the stage of the Folies Bergère or any badly-lit clip joint … but worn to a private party which is celebrating one of the most serious and important bonds in human society, it is unbelievably bad manners. Liz Hurley's dress, like a showgirl's costume, draws the eye directly to the wearer's underwear. It allows no subtlety, leaves no room for the imagination. Its appeal is as direct, crude and vulgar as a lap-dancer's smile. It cheapens its wearer.'

The male point of view, however, was predictably a lot more indulgent. 'There is absolutely nothing wrong with this dress,' argued former lad mag editor James Brown, also writing in the *Mail*. 'If Liz Hurley was some wizened old crow with more lifts than the Empire State building, then it wouldn't be so easy on the eye. But the fact of the matter is she's an attractive young woman going out to enjoy a friend's wedding. What do people want her to wear, mummification bandages? Hurley is saying: "Take a look at these legs," and most guys would say: "Thanks!"'

Stunningly beautiful, 10 years younger than Liz and having just married one of Britain's most eligible bachelors, Lili Maltese could afford to be magnanimous and turn the other cheek at Liz's outrageous bad manners. 'Lili is just the kindest, sweetest person so I think she just puts up with Liz upstaging her,' says Birgit Cunningham.

However, a week later Liz was at it again, appearing topless on a hotel balcony in Cannes in full view of photographers, wearing just a G-string and sunglasses. 'I really wanted to sit on my balcony outside my bedroom, but I could see that there were about five paparazzi standing out there on a rock,' she subsequently explained to *Observer* journalist Andrew Anthony. 'I knew that if I went out on to the balcony I'd be photographed, and I was like: "Well, here I am in the South of France on my bed and I really want to sit outside but if I sit outside it'll be 'Liz flaunts herself for photographers'." And that was really unfair because all I wanted to do was read my book outside my sweaty bedroom. Then I thought: "Well, fuck this," and sat outside and flaunted myself.'

But as a subsequent article in *The Scotsman* pointed out, it really did strain credulity to believe that on her enormous Estée Lauder salary she would be staying in a hotel without air-conditioning. And if she wanted to sunbathe, it reasoned, why couldn't she have kept her top on for once? Rather ludicrously, Liz tried to portray herself in the same article as some sort of shrinking violet. 'I don't go out much,' she said. 'I keep a low profile.' In reality, the fiercely competitive Elizabeth had had her nose put well and truly out of joint by the British media's obsession with a new celebrity king and queen: David Beckham and Victoria Adams. And while she may have claimed that she and Hugh were much happier since the tabloids had turned their attention to Posh and Becks, in truth the only person Liz was interested in seeing on the front pages was herself.

As well as filming her role in *My Favourite Martian* in 1998, Liz also appeared in the movie *Permanent Midnight*, playing Ben Stiller's long-suffering wife. But her acting career suffered a set back when she lost out on a major role in the Austin Powers sequel, *The Spy Who Shagged Me*. The character of Vanessa Kensington appeared only fleetingly and was killed off before the opening credits had finished running. The key female role went instead to the blonde 28-year-old American actress Heather Graham.

The final year of the millennium did not get off to a happy start for Liz. In March 1999, her beloved Alsatian Nico died. She revealed the sad news to Prime Minister Tony Blair in a letter urging him to change the quarantine rules. Lady Fretwell, who runs the pressure group Passports for Pets, of which Liz is a member, said Liz had felt bad about Nico having to do six months quarantine when she brought him back from America. 'She feels she betrayed the dog by putting him in kennels,' she said. According to Henry Brocklehurst, Liz had been 'incredibly attached' to the pet. 'She got Nico when she and Hugh were spending long periods apart and she jokingly admits that she spends more money on that dog than she has ever spent on Hugh,' he said.

The following month she faced more upsetting news when a modelling friend was murdered in a nightclub car park. Cassidy

Chapter 7

Chytraus was just 28-years-old, and had starred with her in a TV commercial for Estée Lauder just ten days earlier. He was stabbed by a psychotic drug addict in San Diego, California, and had been trying to defend his mother when the lunatic knifed him. 'He was fantastic,' said a distraught Liz. 'He was enchanting and we got on terrifically well. This is just the most terrible thing to have happened. I feel so terribly sorry for his mother.'

But Liz also had problems of her own. She was at a major crossroads in her private life. After 12 years with Hugh, their relationship had finally run out of steam.

8 The End of the Affair

In terms of her career, 1999 was very much Elizabeth's year. In May the Walt Disney release *My Favourite Martian* opened, in which she played an obnoxious, untalented TV reporter called Brace Channing. 'I think it's almost always more fun to play a naughty character,' she said. 'I'm having a bit of revenge playing this spoiled and annoying woman. She's out for herself and if you get in her way you get trampled on.' *My Favourite Martian* was followed by *EDtv*, which received favourable reviews in America. But Liz was still aggrieved that people in Britain weren't taking her as seriously as she would like. 'I get livid when people who have never set eyes on me write unjust and pathetic things about me,' she complained. She also launched an astonishingly bitter attack on her fellow Brits, whom she branded 'sad and repressed'. Attending the US première of *Mickey Blue Eyes* with Hugh Grant, she caused consternation by slating her countrymen in front of millions of American TV viewers. 'I don't think English people on the whole like people doing that well and they get particularly cross if you've done OK in America,' she moaned. 'I think we're pretty furious when people do well. I think it is a little bit of jealousy, and I think an

English thing is never wanting to be seen to fail, so a lot of people don't bother trying. And I think I really learned here, it doesn't matter, it's better to try and not make it this time and do it the next time and keep going. And that's a very American thing for us English – sad, repressed people.'

She and Hugh were all smiles at the première, dancing an impromptu tango in a rare show of public affection. But Hugh revealed that they had argued constantly during filming. 'You row like cats,' he said. 'You do with any producer, but especially your girlfriend.' Liz admitted that she had been even harder on Hugh than when they had been making *Extreme Measures*. 'I think I learned to be crueller to Hugh for sure,' she said. 'I was more demanding as a boss, criticized him more, made his life worse.'

In October, she was placed 25th in a survey of top British female earners, with her earnings estimated at more than £2 million. But although her career was going from strength to strength, her love affair with Hugh had hit the rocks. Although they appeared to have survived the Divine Brown incident, in reality there were already cracks in the relationship. It had become increasingly sexless and the truth was that neither Liz nor Hugh was turned on by the other any more. Hugh's arrest for using a prostitute only served to bring into sharp relief the fatally damaging problems between them. But Hugh was not the only one looking for a sexual thrill outside their by now platonic relationship. Liz needed to feel desired, and craved the drug of sex. She got off on the thrill of making love in odd places, with the chances of being found out adding to her pleasure. When she was going out with Thomas Arklie she had

had sex with him in a train carriage at Waterloo station in full view of passers-by.

Liz and Hugh had managed to keep news of their stagnant relationship secret from the Press, but in truth the stalling of the affair and its ultimate breakdown had been on the cards for a long time. 'Hugh is my best friend, I admire him as an actor and, in terms of work, I know what he likes,' said Liz. Nice words, but hardly the stuff of great romantic passion. The truth was that after almost 13 years together the lust had gone. Despite their position as Britain's most famous celebrity couple, Liz was lonely and looking elsewhere for passion. She complained publicly that she had no social life, but the reality was somewhat different. Liz had embarked on a series of affairs while supposedly still with Hugh. For his part, Hugh didn't like going to parties with her because of the attention they attracted. He had been bad enough before the Divine Brown scandal, avoiding visiting Julia Verdin's house because of his aversion to the hordes of people who were invariably there, and his arrest had served to make him even more introverted. But neither did he like it if Liz was seen out with other men, even if they were only 'walkers' like Henry Dent-Brocklehurst.

There was a second problem. Hugh had become seriously depressed. He was disillusioned with acting, something that caused tension between him and Liz. He was exasperated by the media's refusal to forget about his sex scandal and found himself longing for the 'old England' before *Four Weddings and a Funeral*. 'It is nice to be rich, but I have no life,' he said. Elizabeth, in turn, felt frustrated by his lack of enthusiasm for their film company, to which she was passionately committed. She complained to friends that it was hard to get him to enthuse about anything because he was so depressed. She knew it was in both their interests to capitalize on their success while the going was good, and was working around the clock in her role as actress, model and film producer. But she had trouble getting him to commit to things, however good she thought the project was.

Elizabeth is a self-confessed workaholic, whereas Hugh Grant likes to give the impression of cool indifference. Ron Howard, who directed Liz in *EDtv*, was impressed with her dedication and commitment – describing her as 'very intelligent, very professional'. When the movie was released in the summer of 1999, Liz did 86 interviews in one day alone to promote it. And when she and Hugh went on a 10-day holiday to Mustique in early 1999 – their first proper holiday since his arrest – by day eight she had had enough and was ready to get back to work.

Hugh knew she was the driving force behind their partnership, but their conversations were increasingly dominated by business talk. And while it was one thing to be bawled out on the set of a film by your producer, it was quite another to go home together to bed. 'I wake up first thing in the morning and Liz is already up juggling phones and faxes,' he said. 'She loves the business side, and she's damned good at it. Left to my own devices I have the energy of a whelk.' But while Liz enjoyed playing at being a wheeler-dealer in Hollywood, Hugh still despised everything about the place. 'Film industry types never laugh, they want your film to fail,' he observed gloomily. 'London and New York respond well to premières but in Los Angeles they are one-Perrier parties. It's such an insanely competitive town that everyone has to go to bed early so they can be up early and screw somebody over breakfast.'

While Liz was temperamentally suited to the go-getting world of film production, Hugh found that aspect of movies repugnant. His typically English brand of cynicism did not go down well in the US. 'America likes its stars to look as if they are enjoying themselves,' explains Hollywood reporter Marc Freden. 'If Hugh Grant doesn't like it he should quit. There are plenty of other talented actors who can use the work. You don't deserve the good that comes with celebrity if you're not prepared to tolerate, or at least put a brave face on things when they get a bit hairy.'

Liz's and Hugh's different attitudes to work had been much in evidence while they were making *Extreme Measures* in Los Angeles. The crew was amused to see them arriving on set each day, she in a power suit and he in scruffy jeans and faded shirt. Hugh was often to be seen fetching her lunch from the studio's delicatessen. 'Liz is my boss,' he admitted. 'I would be quite happy just being her personal assistant and fetching her cups of tea.' And asked for autographs while they were filming a scene for *Mickey Blue Eyes*, Liz cheerfully signed for her fans while Hugh fled to his trailer.

Had Liz walked away from Hugh during their many previous problems, including her affair with Will Annesley and the Divine Brown incident, it is unlikely her name would merit a flicker of recognition in the US. But now the balance of power in their relationship had shifted. Bluntly speaking, she no longer needed him. She had made it and was now a star in her own right. Every magazine wanted her on its cover, and the days were long gone when she was seen as simply the arm candy of Britain's leading man. In January 1998 their problems were becoming evident. Over lunch at smart, mid-town New York eaterie Fred's, the couple cut a strange and depressing sight. Hunched over a drink, Hugh looked dejected, Liz bored and restless, their misery all too apparent to the upmarket clientele. But as they rose to leave, the entire restaurant stopped in mid-mouthful to gawp at Elizabeth, in contrast, they hardly gave Hugh a glance.

While Grant's career had undoubtedly suffered some damage in the aftermath of his arrest, Elizabeth now had no fewer than three burgeoning careers to pursue. In 2000, the prestigious magazine *Screen International* rated her as the fourth most powerful film producer in Britain. 'Liz was a revelation,' says Jackie Becker, her former New York agent who negotiated the Estée Lauder contract. 'Before I met her, I wondered if she could make it on her own without Hugh. But after seeing her working, I realized it would only be a matter of time before she was much bigger than him.'

Liz yearned for a sex life that would be as rewarding as her work. Liz, the sexual predator who was known in Los Angeles for her dalliances with other women's boyfriends, had long had an eye for pretty, English upper-class, well-dressed 'boys' like Hugh Grant and Will Annesley. In 1998, it was the turn of another English gent to feel the full force of her magnetic charm. Lord John Somerset, the 33-year-old son of the Duke of Beaufort, fitted Hurley's criteria perfectly. The former husband of Diana, Princess of Wales's close friend Cosima Somerset was Liz's date on several occasions, escorting her to Henry Dent-Brocklehurst's engagement party and to fashionable London nightclub Browns.

But it was Liz's next choice of suitor who was to break the mould. Teddy Forstmann was white-haired, had a receding hairline and was almost 60 years old. He was also a billionaire. While still officially living with Hugh, Liz was frequently seen out and about on the arm of the Wall Street tycoon, who was 25 years her senior. Forstmann, who once dated Diana, Princess of Wales, had a penchant for beautiful models and lavished his considerable wealth on Elizabeth. He escorted her to show-business parties and glittering gala evenings in Los Angeles and New York, and whisked her off on a post-Christmas skiing holiday to Colorado in his private jet. Forstmann had amassed his vast fortune by taking over huge companies like Gulfstream and Dr Pepper and enjoyed spending his money. If he wanted to see Liz he would send his plane to collect her and bring her to his luxury home in the Rockies. Liz even stayed with him while she was filming her new movie, *Bedazzled*. Hugh, reluctant to be seen as a cuckold, played down the relationship between Liz and Teddy Forstmann to friends. But those closest to the couple were amazed by her brazen antics. And although Liz's and Hugh's waning romance had been an open secret in show-business circles for years – Hugh had even missed Elizabeth's 31st birthday party, thrown for her by her devoted friend Henry Brocklehurst – friends were dismayed to see her rub his nose in it quite so openly.

Another serious issue in Liz's relationship with Hugh was his absolute insistence that he would not father children for her. He was almost pathologically opposed to the idea of parenthood and had said, 'I have not got a more mature view of it than this: if I was fabulously rich and lived in a big castle and all my children were being beautifully looked after by nannies and appear in their sailor suits for tea – then fine. What I can't think about is a little house in Wandsworth with lots of toys around me and carrying a baby in a papoose on my back. That is not my idea of fun. Selfish? I know it is.' Meanwhile, the ticking of Liz's biological clock was beginning to resound through their relationship. Like many women trying to compete in a man's world, she had put her emotional feelings on hold to pursue her career, but with time ticking away she began increasingly to think about becoming a mum. 'I'm sure I will have children one day,' she said in early 1999. Liz had been spending time with her sister Kate's babies but admitted, 'If I had a child now it would be demented.' However, motherhood was still on her mind and causing her a great deal of soul-searching. She was frightened she wouldn't be a good mother because of the nature of the business she was in. 'How am I going to give children a stable upbringing when I'm so unstable myself?' she said. 'I find it hard to organize getting my legs waxed, let alone arrange nanny schedules. Something has got to give. I would be one of those showbiz mothers with maladjusted, dreadful children because they haven't been there.'

In April, Liz was up to her scene-stealing ways again when she attended the London première of Hugh's new film, *Notting Hill*. Just as in *Four Weddings and a Funeral*, Grant played a bumbling Englishman who falls madly in love with a beautiful American. And just as at the *Four Weddings* première, Elizabeth succeeded in grabbing the limelight from the film's real stars. Hollywood A-list actress Julia Roberts played Hugh's love interest in the film and flew to Britain for the première in

Leicester Square. But for the thousands of fans who had queued up outside – joined by almost as many Press photographers – the 64-thousand-dollar question was would Liz be able to outshine Julia Roberts?

In the end it was no contest. While Roberts wore an elegant, high-necked, pink silk gown by the Chinese American designer Vivienne Tam, Liz flaunted the famous Hurley curves. Her backless, see-through Versace dress left little to the imagination, cut dangerously low at the front and slit at the side from ankle to hip. The next day's papers predictably saw her plastered all over the front pages. She had done it again. Matters were not helped by the fact that when Roberts waved to her fans she had revealed an unshaven armpit. The startling sight served only further to illustrate the difference between the two women.

While the debate raged between the women's pages of that week's newspapers as to whether or not it was right to abandon one's razor, there was one point on which everyone was in agreement: you would never, *ever* catch the perfectly groomed Liz displaying hairy armpits. '"Hair" and "sexy" cannot be synonymous in my book,' she says.

With the obvious similarities between the première of *Four Weddings and a Funeral*, it became evident just how much Liz had changed in the intervening five years. *The Independent* wasn't the only newspaper to comment that she was now almost unrecognizable from the comely wench who had charmed the nation in her safety-pin dress. It contrasted 'Elizabeth I: the healthy, round-faced girl with substantial curves and moderate English good looks' with 'Elizabeth II', whom it said now resembled 'Jackie O. on speed'. The perils of losing too much weight had been made on more than one occasion before. 'Beware English girls who go to Los Angeles to make their name,' said Emma Forrest, writing in *The Guardian* in 1997. 'Arrive a rosy ingenue and look like a 47-year-old divorcee within minutes. The lack of moisture, plus the crash diets, means that every wrinkle is magnified.'

When *EDtv* was released in Britain in November, the *Daily Mail*'s film critic Christopher Tookey also made reference to Liz's new fuller-looking pout – which he described as her 'worryingly bulbous upper lip'. The same month, the *Daily Mirror* newspaper suddenly decided that it had had enough of Liz's propensity for displaying acres of flesh in order to get publicity. It ran a caption next to a photograph of her half-clad breasts, saying, 'The *Mirror* would like to congratulate Ms Elizabeth Hurley on the 5,000th occasion she has attended a party thrusting her cleavage at photographers for no apparent reason other than to appear in the same papers that she regularly claims to despise. *And we are still falling for it.* '

A few weeks after the *Notting Hill* première, Liz and Hugh were back in America. Invited to the glittering launch party of new US journal, *Talk* magazine, they arrived hand in hand. But the evening was to end in humiliation for Hugh when Liz left with another man, leaving him to run along behind. Liz appeared in the magazine's debut edition in August, where she gave an insight into her relationship with Hugh. But her words were a damning indictment of their partnership and revealed that the only thing she now found irresistible about Hugh was his mind. 'We're not like some fabulously happy Adam and Eve all the time,' she said. 'We bicker like mad but it's like arguing with my sister. I've never got bored with him because he's clever.

It's so hard to find a clever man. Easy to find a sexy one, but not one you want to discuss a problem with. I expect we'll be together for ever. Even if, for some bizarre reason, one of us fell in love with someone else, I couldn't cope with not speaking to him every day. I couldn't bear to lose Hugh as a friend.' But as usual, she firmly ruled out marriage. 'That ship sailed, you know, being swept off your feet,' she said tellingly.

Every actress must have a gay best friend and Liz was no exception. But in typical fashion, she had to have two. She had become extremely chummy with Elton John and his boyfriend David Furnish, and attended the 2000 Cannes Film Festival with Furnish instead of Hugh Grant. Later that month she was again out and about with Teddy Forstmann, this time at a New York Knicks basketball game. Liz wore a tight red T-shirt with the slogan PORN STAR IN TRAINING across it – a present from Elton John which predictably got her noticed. *The Sun*'s Marina Hyde posed the question on everyone's lips: 'Refreshing honesty, but what training? She's been hawking herself about in straight-to-video projects for years.'

The same month Liz was photographed with a mystery man on a beach in the Caribbean – sucking a baby's dummy in a bizarre attempt to give up smoking. Within weeks she was on the Italian isle of Capri with yet another man, photographer Sante D'Orazio. And for his part, Hugh had long been raising eyebrows too. While Elizabeth was in the throes of her affair with Will Annesley, Hugh had been out on the town in a Sydney nighclub with Kate Fisher, one of the stars of *Sirens*. And his supermodel co-star Elle Macpherson was wrapped around him at a pre-BAFTAs party in London, and they snuggled up together in the car when they left. At the Cannes Film Festival in 1998 he was photographed kissing his *Mickey Blue Eyes* co-star Jeanne Tripplehorn – a show of affection they repeated at the film's London première a few months later.

Although they had drifted apart, and in May 2000 had not been seen together in public for at least four months, Liz was still reluctant to admit that the affair was over. Tellingly, in an interview given before the split was announced, she was barely attempting to keep up the façade that the romance was still on. 'We drive each other demented half the time, but he really is my best friend,' she said. 'If we don't talk to each other for a day it's torture. And if we split up, I would feel like my brother had died. It takes a lot to come to terms with feeling that way about someone. If you've got it, hold on to it.' But her indiscreet dalliances with numerous men made it impossible. Within days of her comments the couple was forced to admit that the fairy-tale was over. The news that they were putting their romance 'on hold' was released on May 23 in a statement. 'It is a temporary thing,' it said. 'It is a mutual and amicable decision.' Liz was later to describe splitting with Hugh as a 'very long and painful business'. 'After agonizing discussions we both decided we really needed a break to work out how we wanted to live the rest of our lives,' she said.

On the day the break-up was announced, Liz left home wearing her by-now trade-mark white. She looked immaculate in white fake fur jacket and white jeans, and smiled for the cameras. She was accompanied by the ever-loyal Henry Brocklehurst, who helped her fight her way through the Press throng outside the house. Hugh, leaving home for a day's filming on his latest movie, *Bridget Jones's Diary*, appeared equally laid back. 'I'm feeling fine,' he assured reporters. The Hurley/Grant break-up was hot news and had grannies all over Britain sobbing into their hankies. The fairy-tale romance was over and it was the most upsetting news since Torville's and Dean's announcement that they were marrying other people.

Liz and Hugh would carry on living together for the time being, their spokesman said. This was not as unusual as it at first appeared because for the most part they were not even going to be in the same country. While Hugh was filming *Bridget Jones's Diary* on location in England, Liz was still shooting *Bedazzled* in the States. *Bedazzled* was an $80 million remake of the 1967 Peter Cook and Dudley Moore film, which had featured Cook as the devil. In a twenty-first-century twist, the new film starred Liz as a sexy female devil. She had fought off stiff competition from other actresses to get the part, including Madonna. 'I was told by Madonna's agent that Madonna is the devil, which is why she'd be perfect for the role,' says the film's director, Harold Ramis. 'But I was thinking of who was the baddest, most beautiful woman in Hollywood. And I came up with Elizabeth. Elizabeth is witty, worldly and wise. She's very comfortable in her own skin.'

When they started filming, it was soon apparent that Liz was far from comfortable as an actress. Film critic Sean Macaulay visited the set of *Bedazzled* and was amazed at how nervous she was. 'Two things were immediately apparent: her insecurity as an actress and her confidence as a model,' he explains. 'As an actress she is amazingly timid. Brendan Fraser was bouncing about on set, larger than life, joking with the crew, but Liz was nowhere to be seen. She stayed in her trailer most of the time, smoking Marlboro Lights, drinking Diet Coke and talking on her mobile phone. And when she did come out I couldn't help but notice that she would often forget her lines even when they used an autocue for her lines to camera. It was the equivalent of the alcoholic relative in the corner of the room at Christmas – everyone just pretended it wasn't happening. But you could see the crew thinking, "This is day 25 of a 90-day shoot."

The result was that she seemed to get more and more tense with each failed take and her voice became more plummy. And when she started to walk she did that thing where it looks like she's only got one heel. But whatever insecurity she has as an actress, as a model it's the reverse: no problems at all. She is totally confident of her physical effect. When she is posing for pictures she is sensational. For one classroom scene in *Bedazzled* she was wearing a very short skirt. In between takes she would sit with her legs up on the table, well aware of the effect this was having. Members of the crew would mysteriously find reasons to go and move cables when she sat there so they could see if it was true that she never wears knickers.'

Despite the radiant Estée Lauder photographs of Elizabeth that peered out of virtually every magazine, Californian dermatologist Dr Vail Reese revealed that her face bears the scars of teenage acne. As a result, while being photographed or filmed she relied heavily on the skills of both make-up artists and lighting men. 'Her complexion did require extra consideration while she was making *Bedazzled*,' reveals Macaulay. 'She had to be lit very carefully with a powerful key light perched above the camera. It's a cinematographer's adage that you either light for the room or the face, and occasionally let's just say the room suffered.' The hole which Liz had pierced in her nose herself with a safety pin as a teenager also needed to be carefully disguised.

Watching Liz in action on the set of *Bedazzled*, Macaulay saw her coping with the demands of being a Hollywood star. 'She got $500,000 for the film, which is not a huge amount for a lead actress, but she was billed as the co-star above the title,' he says. 'It was a massive step up for her. She was now expected to carry a big Hollywood movie and it proved a lot to handle. It would have helped if she had created better chemistry with Brendan Fraser. A more secure performer would have found ways to bond with their co-star.' But Liz had a powerful ally in her genial director, Harold Ramis. No matter how many times she fluffed her lines Ramis remained serenely untroubled. 'He was literally bedazzled by Liz,' explains Macaulay. 'The crew joked that he was a Jewish rabbit in the glare of a shiksa (gentile) headlight.' And when Liz asked his permission to do a lucrative modelling assignment for an underwear advertisement, Ramis said he would be 'delighted'.

Fortunately, Liz's part did not require Shakespearean ability and her main role was to look as sexy and alluring as possible. 'I wanted to look like a cross between Cruella de Vile and a soft-core porn star,' she said. 'It was amazing to have such a free rein with costumes. Nobody could turn to you and go "I don't think the devil would wear those shoes" because how would they know? There were no rules, no boundaries and it was nice to go berserk on the physical side.' Much of the style she displayed in the film was actually her own, with Versace and Fendi supplying the clothes she liked to wear. Asked in interviews what pact she herself would make with the devil, she didn't hesitate. 'I would want to consume about 12,000 calories a day and never get fat, stay up ludicrously late every night and never look tired and drink like a fish and never have a hangover,' she said.

In June, photographs of her posing provocatively with an enormous python between her legs appeared across several pages of the US *Talk* magazine. In one of the pictures – which were branded 'tacky, downmarket, with more than a nod towards the top shelf' – she was seen suggestively easing the snake towards her open mouth. 'Simulating sex with a snake is utterly degrading and little short of pornography,' reckoned Viv Groskop, in a 'Saint or Sinner' article for the *Daily Express*. 'For someone who is always moaning that no one treats her seriously as an "actress/producer", to use soft porn images to promote herself is hypocritical to say the least.' But Groskop's colleague Heather O'Connor argued that Liz was, in fact, a 'triumph for the modern woman'. 'She is proving that she has the guts and the drive to succeed in a cut-throat celebrity world,' she praised. 'Elizabeth Hurley is a goddess who should be considered a true icon of our age. In our dreary lives, we need women like her to give us the kind of beauty and glamour we can admire and aspire to.'

Although she had been the one to initiate the break-up, Liz missed her relationship with Hugh. 'Even though I felt like I was amputating my left arm, I needed to try life without Hugh,' she said, a touch over-dramatically. 'I was terribly upset at first, and then it seemed fine and we were rather smug about it working so well. But once we told everyone it became much more real and I felt absolutely awful.' Liz had never lived on her own in her entire life. When she left home and moved to London she had lived first with her sister, then with Thomas Arklie and finally with Hugh Grant. And in Los Angeles she had shared a house with Julia Verdin and later William Cash. 'I hate the idea of living by myself, so I'm not sure what will happen here,' she said. 'I think I like splitting up more in theory than in practice. It was extremely difficult and painful because we'd been together since I was 21 – more than a third of my life. In many ways we're perfect for each other, but ultimately we realized that there had to be something lacking because after 13 years together we still didn't really want to get married and start a family. We finally had to acknowledge that that was a bit weird.'

But she denied that their relationship had been a business-only arrangement since the Divine Brown scandal. 'We've loved each other passionately for years,' she insisted. 'Hugh and I could quite easily have stayed together for another 40 years. Our day-to-day life was very easygoing and we provided massive support to each other, which is possibly what we're going to have the hardest time doing without. My hand still wanders towards the phone to call him every five minutes, and it's hard to force myself not to. Hugh and I both laugh and cringe at the same things, worship the same books, love the same movies, eat the same food, hate central heating and sleep with the window wide open. I always thought these sorts of things were vital, but being like two peas in a pod ended up not being enough. I think we'd both been unhappy for some time. Maybe it's a feeling that there may be something more. Our separation is us trying to discover if what we've had is indeed as good as it gets.'

But in August she appeared to paint a far less flattering portrait of Hugh. The US publication *Jane* magazine quoted Liz as saying that her sex life with Hugh had been 'less than adequate'. She said they hadn't had sex since they split up, adding, 'I don't miss it.' Within days Liz was angrily denying that she had said any such thing. 'Hugh Grant is fantastic in bed – he always has been,' she said. 'The article makes me look spiteful and nasty and I'm not.' But she certainly managed to make herself appear spiteful and nasty when she made a snide remark about Marilyn Monroe. 'I'd kill myself if I was as fat as Marilyn Monroe,' she said in an off-guard moment. 'Most of us would kill ourselves if we were as talent free as Elizabeth Hurley,' retaliated American actress Claudia Shear, outraged that anyone should dare to criticize the legendary star. And the boot was on the other foot for Liz a few weeks later when tennis beauty Anna Kournikova branded her 'ugly' after sitting near her at a charity tennis match.

Liz's Hollywood career was at its pinnacle at the start of the new millennium, but within just six months it was threatening to collapse around her ears. She ran into serious trouble when she was accused of strike-breaking by the powerful American union, the Screen Actors Guild (SAG). The union was in the middle of a long-running dispute with the television advertising industry over actors' fees, and Liz was the first Hollywood actor to break the two-month blockade. She crossed a picket line in July to make a TV comercial for Estée Lauder, immediately bringing the full wrath of SAG down upon her. Most of Hollywood's top stars supported the industrial action, and many had donated money to the strikers' relief fund, including Bruce Willis, Harrison Ford, Nicolas Cage, Susan Sarandon, Tom Hanks and Paul Newman. For Liz Hurley to be seen arrogantly defying the union threatened to cost her her entire career.

She was branded a scab for crossing a picket line, and Tinseltown celebrities called for her head. As things turned ugly, Liz claimed ignorance. 'I had no word from SAG in my London home that there was a strike,' she said earnestly. 'And my advertising agency in New York were very remiss in not telling me that there was a strike. But the fact remains they didn't. I didn't know and I had no idea I was crossing a picket line when I did the commercial. If I had known I wouldn't have done it.' The British actors' union Equity remarked that if she had paid her subs and hadn't allowed her membership to lapse, she would have been notified of the US strike as a matter of course.

Liz's excuses failed to cut any ice. 'It's like claiming I didn't know I had shoes on, isn't it?' says Tim Southwell, co-founder of *Loaded* magazine. 'It's not going to wash with anyone.' Liz attempted to carry out some damage limitation by making several fulsome public apologies and donating $25,000 to the strike relief fund. With the heat on, she did what she had always done in times of trouble and turned to Hugh Grant for comfort. In August she escaped the headache of the SAG dispute by accompanying him on a holiday to Sardinia where they joined friends on a boat owned by the Italian designer Valentino. But despite the fact that she was staying on a fabulous yacht anchored off one of Europe's most exclusive islands, Liz appeared far from happy. Shopping in the jet-set town of Porto

Cervo, she wore dark glasses and a sullen expression. The long lenses of the paparazzi were trained on the couple to see if there was any sign of a reconciliation, but although she was spotted giving Hugh a quick peck on the lips there was no sign of them re-igniting their romance.

Liz returned to America to discover that the row with the union hadn't gone away. And if she was still in any doubt as to the depth of feeling against her, it was made abundantly clear when angry strikers besieged the US première of *Bedazzled* in October. Used to being fêted by photographers as she sashayed down the red carpet at premières, Elizabeth was caught completely off guard by the protesters' hostility. Faced by a screaming, yelling mob, waving placards reading LIZ YOU MAKE US HURL! and BEAUTY FADES, HONOUR DOESN'T, Liz looked for all the world like a deer caught in the headlights.

Dressed in tight pink trousers and wearing a clinging sequinned top, she attempted to ignore the fracas by smiling as she walked up the carpet into the Los Angeles cinema. But this served only to further enrage the protesters. 'How dare she stroll in here as though butter wouldn't melt in her mouth?' said one. 'She's a disgrace to the acting profession.' And Hollywood star Tim Robbins warned she would be brought to trial and wouldn't be allowed to get away with it. Liz was facing a hearing about the incident and had been told that if she was found guilty by a jury of her peers she would be expelled from the union and might never work in Hollywood again. Having spent almost 10 years establishing herself in America, it was a frightening prospect. 'Hollywood is a very unforgiving town,' said American screen-writer James Ulmer. 'It may have a short memory as far as someone having a lousy box-office career and all of a sudden they make a million dollars, but it doesn't always have a short memory for behaviour.'

Liz was subsequently fined a further $75,000 by the union and that mercifully appeared to be the end of it. 'She has shaken it off,' says Sean Macaulay. 'The protesters were so ugly and out of work, so militant, that you turned against them. At the time it was a big thing but she said sorry and it's no longer a problem. America is big on forgiveness and you can get away with almost anything if you say sorry.' Liz had indeed made numerous apologies – 'more mea culpas than a penitent at Lourdes' is how the show-business bible *Variety* put it.

But the row served to completely overshadow the launch of her new movie. *Bedazzled* did well at the box office, but Liz's own performance was panned. Praising Brendan Fraser's performance as the love-struck nerd who makes a pact with the devil in order to get the girl of his dreams, film critic Jonathan Ross said, 'Sadly, all his good work is completely undermined by Liz Hurley. I really wanted to like her in the role but she is incredibly, unbelievably, mind-numbingly bad. Liz Hurley cannot act. She has no discernible comic talent and can't even deliver straight lines without them sounding stilted and over-rehearsed,' he blasted. 'It's like being forced to watch a friend who dabbles in amateur dramatics at the weekend suddenly finding themselves on the West End stage. She's way out of her depth and the result is excruciatingly embarrassing. If only Liz would stick to strike-breaking we could all relax.'

Five months on from her split with Hugh Grant, Liz was finding it hard adjusting to life as a 35-year-old single girl. 'I'm dating other men now and it's quite strange,' she said. 'It's a bit weird going on a date at this age.' She claimed she was rarely chatted up. 'For some reason boys are scared of me and they have to be falling over drunk to come near,' she said. 'I think it's really tricky going out with someone famous and because I get followed a lot by the paparazzi it's kind of awful. I guess that's why famous people very often date fellow famous people. For people who aren't in the business it's a really high cost to pay.'

She now admitted that the issue of children had been a major factor in their decision to part company. 'For the past couple of years Hugh and I have talked about having children, but never once did we talk about getting married,' she said. 'I don't know why, but after all that time together it would have driven me demented to have had children with Hugh. So I guess that was really a sign. Now it seems as if time just slipped through our fingers.' However, Hugh's shoes were proving hard to fill. 'He's my best friend and if we're both in London with nothing to do it's nuts not to have dinner together,' she said. Grant had even bought a house four doors away from her in Chelsea.

Although their spokesman had insisted that there were no third parties involved in their split, in reality Liz had already started dating Hugh's replacement. Finally admitting in October 2000 that she was seeing someone new, she coyly referred to him only as 'an American boy'. Rumours were rife that it was either Teddy Forstmann or comedian Denis Leary, her co-star in the film *Double Whammy*. Her married *Bedazzled* co-star Brendan Fraser's name was even bandied about as the Press tried desperately to find out who her new beau was. Many column inches of speculation were published in the gossip columns of the British and American media, but in reality Liz had fixed her sights on someone completely different ...

9 Bing Laden

Liz chose an Elton John concert at Madison Square Garden, New York, to showcase her mystery man to the world. Part of a select group of photographers, journalists and friends allowed backstage, the two had a close-up view of the concert that Elton's fans would have given their right arm for. But as the singer warbled his way through romantic classics like 'Can You Feel the Love Tonight' and 'Sorry Seems to Be the Hardest Word', Liz and her new beau were putting on a floor show to rival his.

Wearing a backless pink top, her trade-mark tight Versace jeans and high-heeled sandals, Liz sat cross-legged on a packing case as she listened to the music. But clearly feeling a bit left out of things, her date summoned her to his side and began rocking her in his arms. And as Elton's songs became more emotional, so did Liz's suitor. To the embarrassment of onlookers, who included celebrity photographers and several journalists, her date became increasingly ardent. In contrast, Liz's response was considerably more reserved. 'He was definitely more into her than she was into him,' observed journalist Chrissy Iley. 'If there was any excitement pulsing through Liz's veins, I think it was a case of Can You Feel the Photo-op Tonight.' Sure enough, photographs of a dreamy-looking Liz, wrapped in the arms of her new love, duly appeared in the next day's papers. Her mystery man was revealed as Stephen Bing, Hollywood playboy and – despite his scruffy appearance – heir to an enormous fortune. Why else would Liz Hurley, voted the sexiest woman in the world, be dating such a plain man? sniped her critics.

It was true that Steve Bing could hardly be said to fit into the pretty boy category that Liz had favoured for most of her life. 'I think beautiful is better for boys,' she once admitted. 'I quite like boys who look like girls, so I like them looking beautiful with nice lines and bones. I don't like great husky-jawed boys. Not too much testosterone.' At a hulking six feet four, and with the hunch-shouldered gait of one who feels too tall, the prematurely grey Bing belonged to her new, preferred category: filthy rich tycoon. At the age of 18, while Liz had been drinking cheap cider and hanging out with punk rockers, Stephen Bing had inherited close to a billion dollars from his late grandfather, New York property magnate Leo Bing. Steve's father, Dr Peter Bing, featured high up on America's rich list and lived with Steve's mother Helen in a beautiful, Colonial-style house high up in the Hollywood Hills, complete with swimming pool and tennis court.

But despite its vast wealth, the family lived a quiet, relatively modest lifestyle, flying economy class and driving around in beat-up station wagons. Until their son's relationship with Liz Hurley propelled them reluctantly into the spotlight, the Bings had been famous only for their discreet philanthropy and charity work. Peter Bing had worked for Presidents Kennedy and Johnson in public health in

Washington and his wife, a tall woman to whom Steve bears a striking resemblance, was a nurse. Their daughter Mary, Steve's sister, works as a social worker in the tough, socially deprived New York borough of Queens.

But although Stephen Bing continued the family tradition of donating generously to good causes, he had also developed a taste for beautiful women and an expensive showbiz lifestyle. Aged 35, he had earned himself a reputation in Los Angeles as something of a playboy. Some even called him a star-fucker. His previous girlfriends included Sharon Stone, Farrah Fawcett, Uma Thurman and Rod Stewart's ex-wife Alana Hamilton. He was fascinated by the movie business and desperate to become a major player in Hollywood.

The couple had been dating for several months by the time of the Elton John concert in November 2000, and Bing had been at her side while she circulated at Oscar night parties in March – a full month before her split from Hugh Grant was announced. But she had, in fact, met him much, much earlier. In the early 1990s, when Liz was living with Julia Verdin in West Hollywood, he would often call in at the house with his friends. But at that time Elizabeth didn't appear to be the slightest bit interested in the gangly, badly dressed 'nobody' and didn't even give him the time of day. 'Steve used to come round with an entourage of six friends who all looked a bit scruffy and wore sports gear and T-shirts and shorts,' recalls Liz's former housemate Birgit Cunningham. 'I never really understood what he was doing in our house because he wasn't as glam as everyone else. He and his friends didn't make any effort to look good and they talked about baseball and football and ice hockey and every sport there was. I didn't know anything about him and I really thought he didn't have any money because he was so scruffy-looking.

'But when I got talking to them they were really funny, a great laugh and they were always going off to do amazing things. But I don't remember Liz talking to Steve when he came round, and I definitely don't have any memories of her chatting with that lot. I would never have put the two of them together because she was so into her English crowd. To be honest, I was a bit surprised when I found out they were dating.' The two certainly didn't appear to have much in common. For one thing, Liz was on record as saying that she didn't enjoy sport 'on any level'. Despite being taken aback to discover that Liz was now seemingly madly in love with the self-same man, Birgit was pleased for her friend. 'When I found out they were dating I was very happy for her because I thought he was such a nice guy,' she says. 'I liked Steve. He was quite straightforward and normal and a lot nicer than the goofy English men she was hanging out with. He was one of those guys you could talk to and he wasn't just scoping the room. He would look you straight in the face and chat and you got the feeling that he was the one person in LA who wasn't after something. A lot of people would try and suss out what you did to see if you were going to be of any use to them. He wasn't like that, so it was really refreshing. I had no idea it was because he was filthy rich.'

Actor James Caan, who is a close friend of Bing's, believes that he deliberately lived like a pauper at that time because he was afraid people would want to cultivate him for his money. 'He didn't want anyone to know he had money,' Caan says. But by 2000 Liz was well aware of both his fabulous wealth and his generosity. When he ate out with friends, Bing was in the habit of picking up the tab for the entire table, and he hired his lawyer friend Marty Singer to help get Liz out of the mess she was in with the Screen Actors Guild.

But if, as many people chose to believe, Liz was attracted to Steve's money, then he for his part was turned on by the idea of dating Elizabeth Hurley. Bing had been trying to break into the movie business for six years and had variously tried his hand as a screenwriter, a director and an actor. At the time he started dating Elizabeth his latest project, producing a remake of the Michael Caine classic *Get Carter* with Sylvester Stallone, had been mocked by critics and flopped at the box office. Liz's Hollywood career, on the other hand, was firmly established and Simian Films was a successful production company. Being seen out with Liz Hurley gave Steve Bing something that no amount of money can buy: credibility.

'I don't really know how seriously he's taken in the film world,' says Tony Broccoli, son of Bond producer Cubby Broccoli. 'There are a lot of producers who have a bit of money and sit back and let other people do the work. The way I looked at it, she was doing more for Bing's image than he was doing for her.' But as far as Liz's old enemy Toby Young was concerned, Liz was out for what she could get. 'I don't think a single person believed that here was a nice couple who had fallen in love,' he says. 'By that time everyone was wise to Elizabeth. They knew that she is not like an ordinary person who experiences ordinary emotions and was just finding a new man and was in the first flush of romantic love. It was just another move on her part in the chess game that is her career.'

Chapter 9

It was arguably a game for Steve Bing too. 'My guess is this in an insecure man, the way that all children of rich and successful parents are,' said Chrissy Iley, writing in *The Scotsman*. 'Why else would be have dated a string of very famous woman if it hadn't been for the validation that comes with a famous name? To prove your pulling power? If daddy's got £400 million, you don't have to pull too hard. You could get anybody who liked money.' And money was something that Steve Bing had bucketloads of. This was a man who had spent the best part of nine years living in a $2,500-a-night suite at Los Angeles's most exclusive hotel, the legendary Hotel Bel-Air. Room 150 is, in fact, a two-bedroom villa, surrounded by lemon trees and bougainvillea and boasting a private roof terrace and open-air Jacuzzi. The hotel's most expensive accommodation, it was Bing's 'bachelor pad' while he awaited completion of his stunning modernist mansion, built high in the Hollywood Hills. The eye-watering room rate at the Bel Air does not include any meals or the liberal tipping which makes the world go round in America. Even with the discount he secured as a long-term resident it cost him several million dollars to live there over the years. But the staff at the Bel Air is nothing if not discreet and Bing could entertain whomever he chose without anybody knowing anything about his business. Not that the Press had been interested in him before he began dating Elizabeth, but when the paparazzi began following the two of them around Los Angeles, Bing knew that he could always escape to the hotel's haven to carry out their affair in privacy and seclusion.

Steve Bing was certainly an attentive suitor. He wrote Elizabeth love letters and took her for romantic strolls along the beach. Their friends believed them to be extremely happy together. Early in their relationship he presented her with a large diamond and sapphire ring, followed a few months later by a solid gold man's Rolex, which she referred to as her 'pimp's watch'. But their relationship was never going to be the love affair of the century. Bing was known in Los Angeles as a serial womanizer who showed no inclination to settle down, and he saw Liz primarily as another pretty girl to have a good time with. 'I think they are two of the same kind,' says one of Steve's friends. 'Steve likes to have fun, and he can. He's single, he's rich, he can do whatever the fuck he wants. I think Liz was a lot of fun for him. She's pretty, she's famous and she loves to have fun too. She's like one of the guys and Steve loved that. I think he was really keen on her. He had a lot of fun with her and that's what the basis of the relationship was. He lived in his place, she lived in hers and they had a lot of good times.'

As well as finding her attractive sexually, Steve Bing was also impressed by the fact that Liz was a successful woman in her own right. 'He was definitely smitten with her and thought it was great to find somebody who was as independent as he was,' says the friend. 'He found her a challenge.' But Bing quickly discovered that there was a distinct downside to dating someone as famous as Elizabeth Hurley. As well as following the couple around Los Angeles, the Press also turned its attention to Steve's family and to the acute embarrassment of Peter and Helen Bing, their private financial affairs were now made public. It was revealed that Peter Bing wasn't adverse to donating up to £10 million a time to charitable foundations and that Stanford University in California boasted a 'Bing Wing' thanks to his generosity. Steve's parents, old money through and through, were appalled that their private philanthropy had been put in the public arena. To their minds, the most important point about giving to charity was that it should be done privately and without ostentation. To see their various bequests listed in the pages of tawdry supermarket magazines was, for them, the very height of vulgarity.

Steve's own bequests were also sifted through and it was revealed that he had donated £600,000 to a child welfare project run by film director Rob Reiner – leading to inevitable remarks that he was trying to buy his way into Hollywood. Having his private affairs, and those of his parents, trawled through by the media did nothing to help a romance that was only in its infancy. There were also other problems undermining the relationship, in particular the fact that Liz did not find Steve Bing as easy to manipulate as she would have liked. She had been used to wearing the trousers in her relationship with Hugh Grant, and was bossy and dominating by nature. But in Steve Bing it seemed she had finally met her match. 'She thinks she can boss people around like she did with Hugh Grant,' said a Hollywood insider. 'I have friends who have worked with her on movies and they told me how she used to boss Hugh around. It was like, "You have to go to the potty now, Hugh." She bosses her gay friends too and I think they love that. They think it's fabulous and divine. But that doesn't cut it for straight guys. Straight guys don't like that kind of personality.'

After splitting from Hugh Grant, Liz had stated publicly that she wanted a man to wait on her 'hand and foot', but Steve Bing was never going to be that kind of guy. He was used to being the one who was waited on: not for nothing had he spent all those years living at the Hotel Bel-Air, with its ratio of two staff for every guest. In March the couple split up but within weeks the romance was back on. Attending a basketball game with him in Los Angeles, Liz certainly gave the impression of being a woman in love. While Steve gave the match between the Los Angeles Lakers and the Portland Trail Blazers his full attention, she went into full-on devoted female mode. She clapped warmly when Bing's team scored, leaned dreamily on his shoulder and gazed deeply into his eyes. For his part, Steve's friends believe he may also have been falling in love with Elizabeth. 'I think maybe he loved her, in his way,' says one. 'I think he loved being with her and loved hanging out with her.' However, by July it was all off again and Liz was seen kissing and cuddling handsome New Yorker Mark Reynolds at a charity polo match in Long Island. Both Steve Bing and Denis Leary were also at the match and Liz found herself in the slightly bizarre position of being photographed in the middle of a group consisting of Reynolds, Bing and Leary – all of whom she had been linked with sexually. She was also photographed with various other men that summer, including singer Bryan Adams, US basketball star Steve Nash and Koo Stark's former husband Tim Jefferies. And she continued to see Hugh Grant, whose pivotal role in her life did not appear to have changed in the slightest.

Although her love life continued to attract more interest than her acting ability, Liz was working as hard as ever. In early 2001 she was busy filming her latest movie project, *Dawg*. The film starred Denis Leary as a selfish womanizer who must apologize to all his previous conquests before he can inherit $1 million and

Liz as the lawyer who must help him. It was her second film with the comedian, neither of which had exactly set the world alight. *Dawg* was an unbelievably lame effort which tested viewers' endurance almost to breaking point, and their previous venture, *Double Whammy*, still hadn't been released in the UK nearly three years on. Liz had become extremely close to Leary, who was married with two children, but the pair denied being lovers. She also landed a £3 million role alongside *Friends* star Matthew Perry in the Hollywood comedy, *Serving Sara*. And she still had her modelling commitments for Estée Lauder, although rumours had been rife for some time that she was about to be dumped.

Evelyn Lauder, wife of the company's chairman Leonard, had described Liz as 'a lady' when they hired her in 1995. But after five years her increasingly colourful private life and habit of posing for overtly sexual magazine photo spreads was causing problems within the family-owned firm. The chairman's niece, Aerin Lauder, was said to favour actress Gwyneth Paltrow for the job, and Leonard Lauder admitted that he had been urged to replace Elizabeth by friends who felt her behaviour had become too tawdry. 'Among my British friends, the people who are in the upper class say, "How can you do this?"' he said. But Lauder had become very fond of Elizabeth and was loath to sack her. On the one hand, he felt that Liz appealed to modern career-women – the company's target market – because Hugh Grant's arrest had made her appear vulnerable and human. But on the other, he acknowledged that posing for suggestive photographs with snakes had led to a mixed reaction in some quarters. 'The men love her,' he said. 'Some women do too, but some respond negatively to her more risqué aspects.'

It was a dilemma that took him many weeks to resolve. Despite his reservations, in the end Lauder decided to renew her contract. 'My head said, "Sure, make a change," and my belly said, "Not yet,"' he said. 'I think it is in the best interests of the company to stick with her rather than change. It's hard not to love her. I think she is beautiful and she is just coming into her own.' Liz was immensely grateful for Lauder's loyalty. 'There have been times when Leonard's been so nice to me that I've cried,' she admitted. She signed a new £2 million contract at the end of 2000 but the writing was on the wall and it was only a matter of time before she would be replaced.

That day moved a great deal closer following her extraordinary appearance at the *Vanity Fair* Oscars party in March 2001, when she turned up with a hot date: former *Baywatch* actress Pamela Anderson. In a brazen display of lesbian chic, the couple paraded past every line-up of photographers, fawning all over each other for the cameras. Anderson, whose breasts were barely contained within a shirt that was unbuttoned to the waist, wore the tiniest miniskirt and looked just about as sleazy as it is possible to look. Beside her anyone would look classy but for once Liz failed to impress. Wearing a dress with a higher than ever split and a plunging neckline, she looked almost as cheap as her date. Evelyn Lauder no doubt choked on her bran muffin when she saw the pictures of the two of them cuddled up together in the next morning's papers.

The spectacle served to demean both Anderson and Hurley because it was such an obvious publicity stunt, contrived to get them publicity. Joan Collins laid into Liz, criticizing her choice of date and advising her to 'get Hugh Grant back'. Being seen arm in arm with 'trailer park trash' like Pamela Anderson had done nothing for Liz's image and, more pertinently, did her no favours with Estée Lauder. And it wasn't just her appearance at the *Vanity Fair* party that was damaging her standing at the company. In April she had peeled off her knickers at Santa Monica nightclub Chez Jay and handed them to an admirer, telling him that she hoped they'd bring him luck. She had also befriended 62-year-old former Mafia crime boss Dominick 'Donnie Slacks' Montemarano, who was keen to forge a career for himself in Hollywood.

Within six months of the Oscars party Liz was ousted as the face of Estée Lauder and replaced by Carolyn Murphy, an American supermodel 10 years her junior. Liz attempted to put a brave face on things, an effort made easier by Estée Lauder's announcement that she would continue to promote its perfumes and make personal appearances in aid of breast cancer awareness, a cause the company supported. 'I couldn't be happier,' she said. 'The new deal works perfectly for me. I'm going to travel a lot more and do many more public events, which I much prefer to sitting in a dark studio all day.' She remained 'besotted with, and grateful to' Leonard and Evelyn Lauder, whom she referred to as her 'surrogate American parents'. But within days she was telling a different story. 'To be honest, I never really wanted to do it,' she told a reporter. But by that time Liz had far more important things on her mind. She was pregnant.

During one of the many 'on' bouts in the on-off drama that was their relationship, Liz had fallen pregnant by Steve Bing. The baby had been conceived in August during a romantic break at Elton John's villa in the South of France. Liz was later to maintain that the pregnancy had been an accident, occurring when antibiotics she was taking interfered with the contraceptive pill. But whatever the circumstances of the conception – which would be a matter of much comment and speculation – Liz was delighted at the prospect of becoming a mum. She had been slowly coming around to the idea of motherhood for some time, and having turned 36 in June she felt that the timing was right for her to have a baby.

But if she had entertained any hopes that Steve Bing would embrace fatherhood in a similarly joyful way, she was to be sadly disappointed. Liz, who had agonized for years about the responsibility and implications involved in having a child, had got herself impregnated by an unreconstructed playboy who was hardly going to relish the news. In her heart of hearts Liz must surely have known this, and it is an indication of the lack of closeness between them that she couldn't even pluck up the courage to tell him that she was pregnant in person. She waited until there was an ocean between them before breaking the news because she knew that he would be horrified.

Steve Bing was at his home in Stone Canyon Road, Beverly Hills on Saturday, September 1 when Liz made her emotional telephone call from London. To his further surprise and displeasure, she told him that she was thinking of keeping the child. Telling her to get on a plane so they could discuss it face to face, it was left to the pregnant Elizabeth to make the tiring 10-hour flight to Los Angeles. When she arrived at Bing's home she faced one of the most unpleasant scenes of her life. While many men, after the initial shock, would have come around to the idea of fatherhood and might even have been pleased, Steve

Bing was not one of them. He made it abundantly clear to her that the pregnancy was unwelcome, and Elizabeth later told her friends that he'd suggested she have an abortion. When she refused, he had apparently suggested that she have therapy – to which she also said no. Steve Bing's reaction to her pregnancy chilled Liz to the bone, and his words left her in no doubt that they no longer had a future together. They split up then and there, and Liz fled straight back to England, where she immersed herself in the sympathy and support of old friends like Henry Dent-Brocklehurst.

As far as Steve Bing was concerned, that was the end of the matter. Elizabeth would either have the baby or not, and if he was subsequently expected to provide for the child financially, then so be it; his pockets were more than deep enough. But Bing had not reckoned on the powerful weapons that Liz had at her disposal. Although they had known each other for more than a year and had shared the most intimate moments, neither appeared actually to know the other at all. Liz had gravely underestimated the strength of Bing's feelings towards her by thinking that he would ever want to settle down with her. 'Despite what has been said about him and his lifestyle, Steve is very old-fashioned and at the end of the day he believes that a child should be brought into this world by a father and a mother,' says a close friend of his. 'You can't control what happens later – divorce or whatever – but at the beginning he would want the parents to be in an exclusive relationship, to which they were both committed. He and Liz never had that. In her delusional head she might have, but it never was for him. She's not the sort of person he would want to have a baby with. Look at the way she dresses. No offence, but anybody who's really secure with their sexuality doesn't always need to have their tits hanging out. There are certain times where it's appropriate, but she's always liked that look. Can you imagine a man saying, "Hi, mum, this is my wife. This is the mother of my children"?'

For the first time in her life, Liz discovered that she couldn't always get what she wanted. But if she had got it wrong about Bing, then he had made a mistake in thinking that she would take his rejection lying down. Liz had more than a decade of media manipulation under her belt and had become a master at public relations and damage control. Hugh Grant's arrest had taught her that even the most calamitous situation could be turned into a potential personal triumph, and she was shortly to turn these skills against Steve Bing.

By the end of October, word was out that Liz was pregnant. A paparazzi photograph, showing her deep in thought and with a red jumper bunched around her far from svelte waist, only fed the speculation. In early November, when she could keep her growing bump secret no longer, Liz issued a short statement confirming that she was pregnant, and saying she was 'delighted' at the prospect of becoming a mother. Standing on the doorstep of her Chelsea home later that day, dressed predictably in white from head to toe, she smiled radiantly for the cameras and accepted flowers from reporters. The Press correctly guessed that Steve Bing was the father, although the 'insider' who reported that the baby had brought the couple 'closer together' was subsequently made to look rather foolish. In reality the pair was barely on speaking terms. Bing showed no sign of having a change of heart and increasingly frosty telephone calls from Elizabeth had done nothing to weaken his resolve. For her part, Liz was determined to go ahead and have the baby. Having failed to get through to him on a private level, Liz now decided to place the whole affair in the public arena. And as news of the impending Hurley baby gripped the nation, she made her killer move.

Liz may have been suffering from morning sickness, but this had done nothing to blunt her razor-sharp instinct for self-preservation. She chose her journalist friend William Cash to write a carefully orchestrated article, revealing that her relationship with Steve Bing was now over and that she was now – *à la* Princess Diana – very much alone. But while she was careful not to say too much herself, she sanctioned friends like Henry Dent-Brocklehurst to talk openly to Cash. 'My friend Elizabeth Hurley looked simply stunning in her new role as Britain's most famous mother-to-be,' Cash gushed, before going on to reveal her 'friends'' contempt and dislike for the bounder Bing. 'Perhaps the best way to sum up Steve Bing's strange behaviour towards Elizabeth is to reveal the joke nickname by which he is now known within certain circles close to Elizabeth – Bing Laden,' he wrote. 'This Californian playboy has no idea of what constitutes chivalrous behaviour.'

Adding his twopennyworth, Dent-Brocklehurst said that whenever he had seen Liz and Steve together they had always appeared to be very much in love. But, he added ominously, it is only when somebody gets pregnant that you discover what a person's true colours were. In the opinion of Liz's friends, Steve Bing's true colour was yellow. He had, they fumed, behaved in a most cowardly and ungentlemanly way. 'There seems to be a dangerously wide gulf of difference between American and British understanding of how to treat a woman when she sits you down and informs you that she is pregnant with your child,' intoned Cash. 'You'd have thought that most men would be ecstatic, as well as flattered, at the prospect of fathering a baby, married or not, with one of the most beautiful and famous woman in the world.'

Elizabeth's friends were further enraged by the fact that Bing seemed intent on carrying on his life as if nothing had happened. 'Incredibly, far from being at Elizabeth's side during doctor's visits, Bing has been seen out partying at his old bachelor haunts in LA and Las Vegas, which certainly used to include various VIP strip clubs,' said Cash. 'Whether that includes the "love grotto" of Playboy Mansion – one of his old favourite hangouts – I have no idea, but his crude insensitivity to the future mother of his child is galling by any standards.' It had been the ever-gallant Hugh Grant who had accompanied Liz to her pre-natal scan at a London hospital. 'I can't imagine for one moment that Hugh is exactly happy about Elizabeth being pregnant by Bing Laden, but he is there for her, just as she has always been for him,' said Cash. Dent-Brocklehurst declared his love for Liz and pledged that her friends would support her 'through thick and thin'.

As Elizabeth's camp congratulated themselves on finding such an clever-dicky moniker for Steve Bing, Cash's *Daily Mail* article was correctly interpreted as a declaration of war. Bing immediately issued a statement saying that they had not been in an exclusive relationship when she became pregnant, and that it was her choice to be a single mother. The clear inference was that

Chapter 9

Elizabeth had been sleeping around. Wounded by what she considered to be a blow below the belt, Liz hit a return serve, saying that she was certain the baby was his, and that she had been 'very much in love with Bing for eighteen months'. She was, she added, 'deeply distraught' by his remarks.

In making his statement, Steve Bing had foolishly ignored Elizabeth's example of letting her friends do her dirty work. While she had cleverly refrained from actually saying anything derogatory about Steve herself, he had put his size-12 sneaker in it. It was an error of judgement that immediately rebounded on him and he now appeared to be more of a heartless bastard than ever. Very few people had any sympathy for him. Even those who liked Steve were astounded by his behaviour. 'I was very surprised at the way he reacted to the baby,' says Birgit Cunningham. 'But guys like him just want to have fun for ever. A lot of the best men on the planet feel that they don't have to ever settle down. Jack Nicholson is their role model.' Liz's friend Tony Broccoli also found the situation difficult to comprehend. 'Why would he go so far as to deny he was the father?' he says. 'If there is anyone you'd want a baby out of wedlock with it, it would be her. She is a very smart, funny, nice person. If there was any chance at all that it could be his baby, why deny it? Why not just wait and see? It's not like he has money problems. The fact that he's so unenthusiastic is strange because lots of guys would love to have Liz as their girlfriend. Although I have to say I don't understand why Elizabeth wanted to make it public either. She was pissed off with him, I guess.'

The British papers described Steve Bing as the biggest bounder since Royal love rat James Hewitt, and there were also comparisons with another of Diana's lovers. 'Rather like an American Dodi Fayed, his money is not his own, but pocket money from his very wealthy father,' said *The Independent on Sunday*'s Jenny McCartney, apparently under the impression that a billion dollars is considered pocket money in America. 'Like Dodi's, the films that he has done have all done rather badly and his greatest achievement is a string of affairs with beautiful women, many of which ended in acrimony.' McCartney considered that Liz would be better off without Bing, and that she and her baby could have a 'splendid time' in London with Hugh Grant, 'who will no doubt be a trouper when it comes to attending PTA meetings, singing silly nursery songs and rustling up Marmite sandwiches'. Hugh was indeed being a swell stand-up guy, accompanying Liz on hospital visits and choosing to stay with her while his London home was being refurbished.

Meanwhile, over in Los Angeles, the latest round in the he-said, she-said war of words was under way. One of Bing's female friends gave an interview accusing Liz of being a gold-digger who had tricked him into making her pregnant in order to get her hands on his money. Brenda Swanson, an American bit-part actress, claimed to be speaking with Bing's full permission because he wanted her to put the record straight. Steve, she said, felt deeply betrayed at being conned into fatherhood and was bewildered by Elizabeth's decision to make her pregnancy public. 'People think what she has done is really trashy,' bitched Swanson. 'What she's done to Steve is disgraceful. She is the sort of woman who gives other women a bad name. Her name is mud here now.' Swanson said Bing had not even been particularly serious about Liz. 'He was never going to marry her,' she sniped. 'She was nothing special to him and he made that clear. The Pill is 99.9 per cent effective. It seems extraordinary that she was with Hugh Grant for 13 years and never had a baby, but it happens now with the $400 million man.'

Although Steve Bing subsequently filed a defamation lawsuit against Swanson, whom he said had no authority to speak on his behalf, Liz strongly suspected that he had sanctioned her remarks. She was furious at what she considered his 'monstrous' behaviour, and was further embarrassed by Swanson's claim that she had a reputation for being 'adventurous and quite kinky in the bedroom'. Liz, who once admitted 'I am usually in the middle of high drama – gossips and scandals and talking', was once again the centre of attention. 'It has all become rather like a high-society version of the *Jerry Springer Show*, with the badger-faced Bing shuffling on stage every so often to receive a resounding booing,'considered Jenny McCartney, writing in *The Sunday Telegraph*. *The Guardian*, meanwhile, likened the situation to a schoolyard fight. 'If the Hurley/Steve Bing spat were the playground squabble that it increasingly resembles, you would have to say that Hurley's gang started it,' said its writer Jane Shilling.

Bing's lawyers were said to be busily compiling a list of men they suspected of being the father of Elizabeth's child. And Steve was determined to undergo a DNA test to prove he was not the baby's father. In the face of such unpleasantness, Liz couldn't stomach spending any more time than she had to in Los Angeles. Despite having just signed a year's lease on a house close to Steve's home in Bel Air, she remained in London. 'I'm certainly not having the baby in America,' she said. 'In Britain, I have people who I know with me and care about me. I have people I can trust. Sadly, I do not feel that is the case any more with LA.'

But the increasingly public slanging match was far from being over. A few days before Christmas, Liz took her battle against Bing up a gear by going on American television. Liz, who was by now six months into her pregnancy and visibly with child, gave a performance on the NBC breakfast show that was reminiscent of the late Diana, Princess of Wales's infamous *Panorama* interview. 'He was great and I adored him,' she said of Bing. 'We were happy together and certainly when the baby was conceived it was in absolute happiness and we were very loyal. So anything else that's been said about that is nonsense. He was so lovely when we were together – could not have been nicer. I loved Stephen enormously during the eighteen months we were together. Unfortunately it all sort of got silly. It would be horrible to have to do it legal and nasty and I hope it won't come to that. And I am sure it will not – we are both too nice.'

But this was by now wishful thinking. By insisting on playing the whole story out in the public arena, Elizabeth had alienated Steve Bing for good. 'I think she was totally crazy about Steve and she thought she was going to get him,' says a friend. 'And if she hadn't made it all public, perhaps he would have come around to the idea of the baby. I know that he would have taken care of the baby and done whatever she wanted. But her ego is so huge that it was a big slap in the face for her when Steve didn't immediately fall down at her feet. He wasn't threatened by her, or scared or intimidated and that really pissed her off. She wanted to have the kid and that's her choice but she shouldn't have tried to pressure Steve by putting it in the Press. She should have just kept quiet. Nobody needed to know who the father was. The biggest mistake she ever made in her life was telling the media.'

That their son should suddenly be the focus of so much media speculation did not sit well with Peter and Helen Bing either. 'Steve's parents are very private, very elegant people,' said the friend. 'They are big in philanthropy and that's it. This has been beyond embarrassing for them. It's hideous. Mind you, that's what you get when you go out with somebody like Liz, who's totally self-promotionalist. The way she plays the Press is terrible, but it's her one claim to fame because God knows her movies aren't doing anything. All she had to do was come out and say: "Please stop calling the man who is going to be the father of my child Bing Laden." She could have come out as a lady and said: "This is a private matter, I'm sorry it's got so carried away and I beg you all to please stop saying anything humiliating about my child's father." But she never did. She had to go on NBC – when she didn't even have a film to promote – just so people would see her side. Shame on her.'

Liz told NBC that she was coping with the situation by focusing on the baby. 'One's sanity and reason is sort of saved by the fact that something very nice is going to ultimately happen,' she said. She also paid tribute to Hugh Grant. 'He has been absolutely the best,' she said. 'He is the best friend to me.'

Few people believed her when she said she hadn't meant to get pregnant. 'Elizabeth would have the world believe that getting pregnant was an unfortunate accident,' says Toby Young. 'Yeah, but the guy that impregnated you happens to be a billionaire.

Coincidence?' But regardless of what people thought, Elizabeth was in the unenviable position of facing life as a single mum. 'Liz wanted people to think of her as a smart woman and not just all tits and teeth but then she went and got herself pregnant,' says Hollywood reporter Marc Freden. 'People thought either a.) "There's another one who was too stupid to see through this man" or b.) "She was too stupid to protect herself" or c.) "She tried to get her hooks into a billionaire and it all blew up in her face." None of those may be true, but whatever way you look at it, it has set back the cause of women in business. In this day and age, I don't care who you are, use a condom if you don't want to get pregnant.'

It seemed that everyone had an opinion on the matter. Not since the Immaculate Conception had a pregnancy attracted so much attention. The *Daily Mirror* even went so far as to print a 'wanted' poster of Steve Bing on its front page, accusing him of 'crimes against Ms Elizabeth Hurley'. Referring to him as a 'sleazeball', the paper published his office telephone number and urged its readers to call and berate him – which they did. Bing responded by filing a multi-million-pound lawsuit against the paper, claiming libel, invasion of privacy and emotional distress. His lawyer, Marty Singer, revealed that Bing feared for his personal safety after receiving death threats from callers with British accents. 'It was a very reckless thing to do,' said Singer. The paper later published a full-page apology under the headline 'We're Sorry, Steve', in which it grovellingly listed Bing's many philanthropic acts and humbly apologized for writing 'mean-spirited and inaccurate' articles about him. But, by coincidence, the apology just happened to be next to an article about how Americans don't understand irony.

Chapter 9

Liz was also having problems in the shape of one Petar Mihajlovic, a 32-year-old Yugoslavian whom she accused of stalking her. He had been hanging around outside her Chelsea home for weeks and had allegedly sent her abusive letters. It would have been upsetting at any time, but at nine months pregnant Liz was particularly freaked out by his attentions. Intervening on her behalf, Hugh Grant made a complaint to the police and on the very day that Liz was making her way to hospital to give birth, Mihajlovic was arrested outside her house.

Liz had longed for a mummy's boy who would 'sit on my knee all day and tell me he loves me', and shortly after midday on April 4 she got her wish. She named her new son Damian Charles Hurley and both mother and baby were said to be happy and healthy. Liz joined the ranks of the 'too posh to push' brigade by opting to give birth by Caesarean section at London's exclusive Portland Hospital. Her sister Kate was by her side in the delivery room and cut the baby's umbilical cord. Damian weighed in at 7 lb 2 oz and, as word spread, Liz's room filled up with flowers and cards from friends and well-wishers. But from Steve Bing there was not a word. Six thousand miles away at his home in California, he posed for photographers but pointedly failed to offer his best wishes or ask how the baby was.

10 Earth Mother

As befitting his status as the offspring of one of the most photographed women in the world, Damian Hurley's birth prompted one of the fiercest magazine bidding wars in history. At one stage, an unprecedented £1.5 million was on the negotiating table as British magazines *OK!* and *Hello!* bid feverishly against their American rivals to secure exclusive photographs of Liz and the baby. Mother and son were considered such hot property that the magazines knew they could more than recoup their money by selling the pictures on around the world. London's most fashionable baby boutiques were also queuing up to get Liz to promote their products and freebies ranging from cashmere bootees to pushchairs were arriving at her Chelsea home almost by the hour.

Everybody wanted to know what the baby looked like but Liz was determined to keep him out of the public eye until a magazine deal had been struck. So when she left hospital five days later, she did not return to her London house. Neither did she do what many new mothers might do and go to stay with their mother. Instead, Elizabeth opted for the secluded luxury of Sir Elton John's £5 million mansion near Windsor. In true diva style, she was collected from the hospital by blacked-out limousine and driven the 25 miles to the singer's home in the Berkshire countryside. Elton and his partner David Furnish were waiting to welcome her inside and assured her that she and the baby were welcome to stay as long as she liked. 'David and I are very lucky because we are in a position to help people who are close friends,' said Elton. 'We try to stick as closely to Elizabeth as possible, because it's a very vulnerable time for her.'

Liz spent seven weeks hiding out at the singer's home. Her decision owed as much to her desire not to be pictured looking fat as to anything else. Having gained almost four stone during her pregnancy, there was no way she wanted to subject herself to the unforgiving paparazzi just yet. She was, in her own words, the size of a tank, but at Elton's home she was fully protected from even the longest camera lens. There she could take long walks in the grounds and work out in the pool and gymnasium to her heart's content. Elton's team of chefs was also on hand to prepare low-calorie meals to help her lose the pregnancy pounds.

Liz had fallen immediately in love with her son and when her sister Kate placed him in her arms for the first time had announced, 'I want another one.' But despite her elation at becoming a mother, the bitter rift with Steve Bing was far from over. She had pointedly left his name off the baby's birth certificate and he had made no attempt to contact her. Right up until the moment she gave birth, Liz had hoped that he would change his attitude towards her and their child but his cool reaction to Damian's birth made her realize it was not to be. Asked what he thought of the name Elizabeth had chosen, he looked down his nose and sniffed, 'I'm not bothered.' With that withering response, Liz knew all hope was gone. And things were about to get even more unpleasant. Bing still appeared convinced the child was not his, although Liz knew otherwise. It was also evident to everyone who set eyes on him that Damian was the spitting image of Steve Bing. Indeed, so striking was the resemblance that a DNA test would now be merely a formality, but on the other side of the Atlantic, Stephen Bing was determined to have it done.

For her part, Elizabeth was equally determined not to go through the 'humiliating' and, to her mind, wholly needless experience of having her son tested. But a fortnight after Damian's birth Bing took legal action, forcing her to comply with his wishes. He issued proceedings in the Family Division of the High Court in London, compelling her to submit a sample of the baby's DNA for comparison with his own. The papers were served on Liz at Elton John's house. 'Now that Ms Hurley has had her baby, Mr Bing is anxious to establish beyond any doubt who is the baby's father,' explained his spokeswoman. 'If it is proved that Mr Bing is Damian's father, he would wish generously to support him and to be involved in his upbringing.' Liz was furious that Bing had seen fit to resolve the paternity issue in such a public manner, but to her frustration there was nothing she could do about it. Her sister admitted that Liz was 'extremely distressed' by his behaviour. Elton John attempted to cheer her up by giving her and Damian the use of his villa in France where she could continue her postnatal convalescence in peace, but it was a frustrating and challenging time for her emotionally.

Chapter 10

As he had initiated proceedings in the British courts, Steve Bing was required also to undergo his DNA test in Britain. On 18 June 18, 2002, he flew into London's Heathrow airport and stepped on to the tarmac just long enough to provide a blood sample. He then turned around and boarded a plane straight back to California. By that time, of course, the test had become laughably redundant as the first pictures of Damian had been published in a British newspaper, showing, as conclusively as any test, that Stephen Bing was his dad. The test provided the final proof and Elizabeth was vindicated. Although it could hardly be said that she had emerged with her honour unblemished, on the matter of Damian's paternity she had been exonerated. Bing, however, hoist with his own petard, now looked a rat for having ever doubted her virtue.

Bing said he was pleased with the result and was looking forward to being part of his son's life. 'He has always said he would be a generous father,' said his spokesman. It was reported that under Californian law, Bing could be forced to hand over up to 28 per cent of his income in child support, entitling Liz to as much as £480,000 in annual maintenance. Damian could also be entitled to a slice of his father's inheritance. But Liz told her friends and family that she didn't want Bing's money. As far as she was concerned, Bing's new-found interest in their son was too little, too late. Her £2 million-a-year contract with Estée Lauder meant that she was more than capable of providing for the baby herself, which she fully intended to do. 'While he's a child, Damian will be brought up in my income bracket,' she says. 'I will very much be the provider. I'm not mega-rich but I've got plenty of money.'

A few days after Damian's paternity was settled, an exultant Liz ended her period of self-imposed exile by attending a charity ball at London's Grosvenor House hotel. Arriving on the arm of David Furnish, who fast appeared to be replacing Henry Dent-Brocklehurst as her favourite walker, her appearance drew gasps of admiration from onlookers. It was the first time she had been seen in public since she'd had the baby and Liz had orchestrated her debut with the utmost precision. The hours that she had spent exercising and denying herself fattening foods now paid dividends and her stunning, full-length, white silk satin Angel Sanchez gown showed off her voluptuous post-pregnancy curves to perfection. Once again, she was letting her choice of clothes speak for her. Displaying an enviable cleavage, which had returned to its glory days of the *Four Weddings and a Funeral* première, the dress said, 'Steve Bing, eat your heart out.' And to the battalion of Press photographers it yelled, 'I'm back!'

Meanwhile, in America Stephen Bing was facing accusations that he'd fathered a second child. The American billionaire Kirk Kerkorian claimed Bing was the real father of his wife's four-year-old daughter Kira. Kerkorian, the 85-year-old owner of MGM film studios, had been married to Kira's 36-year-old mother Lisa Bonder for just one month and was fighting a bitter divorce. And after allegedly having an associate trawl through Bing's rubbish and remove a piece of dental floss from which his DNA was extracted, Kerkorian announced that he was 99.993 per cent positive that Bing was the child's father. Steve, who had enjoyed a brief fling with former tennis pro Bonder, admitted there was a possibility the child could be his, but reacted furiously to people going through his garbage and issued a $600 million writ against Kerkorian, claiming invasion of privacy. This did not stop the Press dubbing him 'The Sperminator', however, or the *New York Post* from ridiculing him with a cartoon showing a park littered with baby Bings.

Reading about it over breakfast at Elton John's house in Windsor, Elizabeth had felt sorry for Steve and decided to give him a ring. It was the first time they had spoken since their son's birth but the conversation turned sour when Bing brought up the subject of Damian's name. Why, he asked her, had she chosen to call their son after the child from *The Omen*? If it was her way of having a laugh at his expense by making out that she had given birth to the devil's spawn, then it was hardly fair on the child. Liz insisted that Damian was a favourite name of hers and that she had intended no such thing. But Bing was not convinced and pleaded with her to change the baby's name to his middle name, Charles. Liz refused and the couple ended their conversation on bad terms. Their son's name remains a bitter bone of contention between them to this day. 'Steve really wants her to change the child's name because he doesn't want the child to be made fun of,' says a close friend. 'She says she loves the name and that it's a very English name, but it has a lot of connotations in America with the *Omen* films. I know Steve's sad that she won't change it because he thinks it's a shame to put that name on a child. But Liz is really selfish. Before she had the baby all she could think about was herself, and she hasn't really thought about how all this animosity is going to affect him years down the line. One day he will read all these horrible things that she has said to the Press, and Steve is really upset about that.'

Steve Bing was also irritated about Elizabeth's decision to

pose with their son on the front cover of *Harper's Bazaar*. She tied up an exclusive deal with the American magazine after *Hello!* and *OK!* magazines dramatically withdrew their offers. The two publications set aside their bitter rivalry to make a stand against what they considered to be the increasingly outrageous amounts of money demanded by greedy celebrities. 'The last 10 months have been a very sad and hurtful time, but in Damian I have such a glorious gift to comfort me and make everything better,' she told the magazine. 'Damian was unplanned but not unwanted. I think the best things that happen to you are preordained. It's fate.' She said she planned to raise her son to respect his father. 'There's a child involved here, so this cannot be about mudslinging,' she added. 'I wouldn't dream of speaking about Damian's father in any other way than respectfully. If you've been brought up not to sink to the lower level of humanity then you don't.' It also helps, of course, if you have friends who are prepared to do your dirty work for you and Liz's pals were happy to contribute to newspaper stories about the bounder Bing Laden.

For Steve Bing, the *Harper's* photographs had provided his first proper look at his son. But he was distressed to see their child vulgarly plastered all over the media. 'Steve finds it upsetting that she lets the baby be photographed,' says a friend. 'He thinks it's a shame because he's always felt that you shouldn't use children for self-promotion. Liz is using the baby as an accessory to get publicity because she doesn't have any hit movies. It's pathetic.' For her re-invention as devoted earth mother, Liz had dispensed with the services of pushchair or pram and instead chose to lug the increasingly large Damian around in her arms.

Whether she was being photographed at the airport heading for Los Angeles, or flying in and out of New York on Concorde, he was always clasped to her bosom, the pair of them dressed in her new preferred uniform of white and cream.

But while Liz's clothes were making her appear whiter than white, Hollywood was abuzz with yet more tawdry rumours about her sex life. In July, an article appeared in the respected American magazine *Vanity Fair*, alleging that she had taken part in a three-in-a-bed sex session with Bing and another woman. The sensational accusation, revealed by one of Bing's friends, heaped more damage on Liz's already tarnished reputation and served further to damage her standing in America. 'They had a threesome in Vegas, so she must have known it wasn't an exclusive relationship,' revealed the pal, exhibiting a flair for short but devastating asides. Ironically, Liz had been asked in an interview in August 2000 if she would ever take part in a three-in-a-bed sex session, to which she had replied, 'I think I'm unlikely to – ever.' But now everyone was wondering if she had changed her mind about three being a crowd. 'That certainly happened and I don't think it was just the once either,' says a friend who knows them both. 'That's one of the reasons Steve liked her so much. She was really fun. Steve's a guy and what guy wouldn't want to go to bed with two gorgeous girls? It isn't so shocking. We're not living in the Middle Ages here. I don't know who the third party was, it was probably someone in Vegas.'

According to the friend, the couple's spicy sex life was common knowledge among their circle in Hollywood. 'It's no big secret,' says the pal. 'You hear about that sort of thing going on all the time, but no one makes a fuss about it. It's not a big deal.' Someone who is in a position to know more than most people on the subject is Liz's former lover William Annesley. But he says he would be very surprised if the allegations of a three-some were true. 'I would think it is extremely unlikely and if I was a betting man I would put money heavily against it,' he says. 'I think that was a smear as there is absolutely no way in hell Liz would put herself in that situation. It would be too dangerous and I just think she's way too clever for that.'

Her former flatmate Birgit Cunningham agrees. 'I don't think she would have taken a gamble like that,' she says. 'Because of their money, guys like Steve Bing are the subject of attention from tarts and prostitutes and wouldn't know a lady if they saw one, quite honestly. They just don't know what real women are all about. I should think that they would jump to the conclusion that just because Liz is gorgeous and sexy and wears a certain kind of clothes, she'd behave the way that the other girls do. But I guarantee she didn't.' Whatever the truth of the three-in-a-bed allegations, the damage had been done and Liz's image had become a little more tarnished. Not for the first time, Leonard Lauder found himself drawn into the fray, and once again he loyally defended Elizabeth to the media. 'I am in no way judg-mental about her private life,' he said. 'She's been rather open about that with me. I do not subscribe to the notion that everyone is as pure as the driven snow. If there were no lies there'd be no sex.' Liz's rumoured affair with the married actor Denis Leary was dragged up again and Steve's sister Mary broke the family's vow of silence to claim that her brother had been 'reproductively taken advantage of'. 'He has been snookered into being a parent,' she fumed.

The *Vanity Fair* story re-ignited the war of words between the two camps. It was the view of Elizabeth and her friends that the article had clearly been written with the close co-operation of Steve Bing. Certainly several of his friends had been wheeled out to present a flattering portrait of him, while denigrating Liz. She refused to comment on the threesome allegations, saying only, 'I'm not going to refute insanely inaccurate, untruthful stories.' But privately she hit back with an article of her own, penned by her chum William Cash for the London *Evening Standard*. 'It seems sad that a man she once adored has turned out to be her tormenter,' wrote Cash. And in a thinly veiled threat to Bing, he added ominously, 'She has a few choice shots up her sleeve if she should ever choose to chuck them.'

In August, Liz flew to Los Angeles to promote her new movie, *Serving Sara*. She took four-month-old Damian with her, prompting speculation that he might be introduced to his father. However, with the publication of the *Vanity Fair* article, relations between her and Bing had deteriorated to such an extent that in the end they were unable even to agree on the basics of how or where any meeting should take place. The biggest obstacle was Steve Bing's total insistence that, while he was more than happy to see the baby, he did not, under any circumstances, want to see Elizabeth. 'He would love to see the baby but he doesn't want to see the baby with her and because of that her ego is bruised,' says one of Bing's friends. 'She won't agree to let Steve see the baby without her being there. Her attitude is they come as a pair.'

The couple can still not agree terms for the all-important first meeting and at the time of writing Bing has yet to see his son. For one thing, he doesn't trust Elizabeth not to tip off the Press about the rendezvous. 'He will see the baby, but in secret,' says a friend. 'It will be a personal thing and I can promise you she won't be in the room. A nanny or somebody will have to bring the baby over to see him because he doesn't want to see her. I'm sure she calls him once in a while but Steve just wants nothing to do with her. They are not speaking. They communicate through lawyers and there's no sign of things improving.' The pair is also at loggerheads over Liz's refusal to have their son circumcized. 'Steve wants the baby to be circumcized. It's a health issue and everybody does it here,' says the friend. 'It's a man thing. But Liz's attitude is "I'm English, we don't do that thing here." She's trying to do the opposite to what he wants.'

The painful arguments with Steve Bing have been offset by the happiness of becoming a mum. 'Motherhood has been a huge learning curve, but it has been a nice thing as it happens,' she said. 'I do everything I possibly can to make Damian happy. I don't think being a mother has changed me, it has added to me. I just feel much, much happier. All I secretly want to do is go home and play with Damian. I just love having him in my life. It really reminds you of what's important and what brings you great joy. I had absolutely no idea that it could possibly be this lovely.' But while no one doubted the sincerity of her love for her child, her next remarks were to make her the subject of much ridicule. 'I put on a pinny as soon as I get home,' she said. 'I love sterilizing his bottles. It's brought out the housewife in me I never knew existed. Oh! I love to iron his little romper suits. I don't think I've ever ironed anything in my life. I didn't even know I had an iron. I love doing his little laundry.'

Chapter 10

The *Daily Mirror*'s Matthew Norman was the first to stick the boot in. 'Obviously on Planet Liz, domestic drudgery was something previously only done by other people,' he said. 'In the real world Liz wouldn't actually last five minutes coping with the problems most single mums have. The only reason she knows her arse from the elbow is because she is so far up her own.' Others felt that the time she'd spent working out in the gym in a bid to get in shape might have been better spent getting to know her new baby. Even her old friend Debra Holder found the concept of Liz as a mother hard to get used to. 'Me and Liz used to hate children,' she says. 'She used to say, "I can't stand kids, they're little buggers and they just get in the way." Neither of us was maternal and we wouldn't even hold our friends' babies. I never thought she'd have a baby.'

In August 2000, *Serving Sara* was released in America, where it was promptly savaged by the critics. 'As a child I thought pure hell meant eternal agony in the flames of Satan but now I know it is looking at your watch and realizing *Serving Sara* isn't even halfway through,' said a reviewer for the *Washington Post*. But there were a few crumbs of comfort to be had and at least one reviewer considered that Liz's performance was not at all bad. 'Maybe Elizabeth Hurley is a better actress than anyone gives her credit for,' said California's *Orange County Register*. 'Even in an extraordinary unfunny bit of cinematic dross such as *Serving Sara*, she always manages to look like she's having a swell time. Hurley's infectious delight is the one saving grace in this unspeakable snooze and, considering the circumstances, quite possibly the acting feat of the year.' Film writers complained about the startling lack of chemistry between Liz and her co-star

Matthew Perry, accusing Perry of looking 'puffy and bored'. Liz also had to suffer the ignominy of the movie going straight to video in the UK.

Her modelling comeback was significantly more successful and with her unfailing knack for grabbing the limelight, she ensured it was suitably dramatic. Appearing in the glossy style magazine *Pop*, she wore a black rubber swimsuit and patent 10-inch high stilettos. Her hair was brutally slicked back and she was holding on to gymnasium rings for support. For some reason *The Guardian*'s Dea Birkett considered that this represented some kind of modern-day model of motherhood. 'Just because a woman has given birth, she shouldn't be swathed in flowery prints,' she wrote. 'You can be maternal and mean. As a working single parent, she's an example to us all. I can think of no other high-profile, sexy, single woman who proudly confirms that you can be successful and bring up baby on your own.' But quite how raising a child equates to posing in a rubber swimsuit while clinging on to gymnasium rings for dear life is anyone's guess.

What was truly remarkable, however, was how slim Liz appeared in the photographs. The dominatrix get-up left no room for so much as an ounce of spare fat and although it had been just 12 weeks since Damian's birth it was clear that Liz had managed to lose every single pound she had gained during her pregnancy. In fact, she had lost an amazing 53 pounds in only two months which, she admitted, had 'almost killed' her. But the way she saw it, she had no choice. 'Being able to squeeze myself into tiny clothes is how I make my living,' she pointed out. She lost the pounds by sticking to a strict diet of steamed fish, plain brown rice, oatcakes and vegetables. She had also managed to avoid getting unsightly stretch marks by rubbing her breasts and stomach with baby oil twice a day during her pregnancy. 'Losing the weight was mostly iron will,' she admitted. 'I made it my mission to get back into shape. I exercised more than I ever have in my whole life.' The magazine's editor Katie Grande praised Liz's commitment to her job. 'We did a rain sequence and we pelted her with freezing water for hours. Not a word,' she said. 'She's so hungry to get it right she'll do anything. She really is one of the most fastidiously hardworking people I've ever done a shoot with.' In the accompanying interview, Liz claimed to have no regrets about her relationship with Steve Bing. 'I have Damian and I wouldn't give him back for all the tea in China, so no, you can't regret the past,' she said.

He may not have met his son, but Steve Bing was determined to set up a trust fund for Damian's future. Liz, however, was against the idea and refused to touch the £100,000 he sent to pay for any private health care the child might need. In December she even went to court in a bid to stop him giving her money. But after a private hearing in front of a judge at the High Court in London – proceedings which had been brought by Steve Bing – it was agreed that he would pay £100,000 a year in maintenance until Damian's 18th birthday. Liz's critics reckoned that she had at last got what she wanted but, in a surprise move, she announced that she didn't want the cash. 'The money is not wanted or welcome,' she said. 'I have always made it perfectly clear to Stephen Bing that I don't want any financial help. However, it appears that one cannot stop someone trying to give you money. Fortunately one can refuse to accept it. This I have done. Mr Bing states that the financial provision in the court order was "by consent". It was not by consent; it was opposed by me in court. Damian and I are managing very well by ourselves.'

Liz could hardly be said to need Bing's money. Wealthy in her own right, she had just forked out £500,000 for a country retreat in the Hampshire village of North Waltham, as a place for her and Damian to escape the pressures of fame. She named the farmhouse Monkeys and, realizing that it would be unoccupied for long periods while she was in London or America, she invited her widowed mother to live at the house full time. Whatever her motives, turning down Steve Bing's money was a shrewd move on Elizabeth's part as she now held the moral high ground and could no longer be accused of being a gold-digger. Brian Reade, writing in the *Daily Mirror*, said Liz had made his Christmas with her 'message of hope for all mankind'. 'She has turned the tables on a powerful Yank, who did what America does to all foreigners, charmed her, screwed her, then left her to rot as he moved on to screwing someone else,' he wrote. 'And now she has said: "Screw you too." Now tell me why the rest of the world can't give the same message to George Bush.'

But her detractors still weren't happy. 'She can't take a dime from him, or it would look like she did it to get the money,' says a Hollywood insider who knows her and Bing. 'She's embarrassed now, which is why she's taking such a stand. But she knows the child will always be taken care of because that's the way Steve is. Steve's a good boy. He does the right thing. The child will have a secure future financially.' The trust, set up by the High Court, is in Damian's name and Bing will continue to pay into it until at least 2020. If Liz chooses not to use the money, her son will inherit close to £1.8 million on his 18th birthday. Despite everything, Liz remains hopeful that her son will be able to have some kind of a relationship with his father. She has tentatively suggested that Steve Bing might be able to act as some kind of an 'uncle' figure in Damian's life, and she still wears the gold Rolex watch that he gave her.

Shortly after the court hearing, Liz left Britain for the winter jet-set haven of St Moritz for a spot of skiing and partying. Doing her best Julie Christie impersonation, she took Damian on a sleigh ride through the Swiss snow, the pair of them wrapped in matching cream outfits and nestling cosily under a fur blanket like a scene from *Dr Zhivago*. Hugh Grant joined her at the resort a few days later and was seen pushing Damian's pram through the snow, once again prompting speculation that they might be getting back together. Liz has admitted to her friends that she finds being a single mum lonely, and often thinks about what she had with Hugh. The fairy-tale possibility that the pair could be reunited has been mooted on and off ever since their split. 'Hugh is Dick Decent and Liz will only finally recognize him as Mr Right when she has exhausted Hollywood's endless supply of Mr Wrongs,' said Yvonne Roberts, writing in *The Independent on Sunday*. Grant's declaration in April 2002 that he still loved Liz and continued to dress to impress her shifted the rumours up a gear. He also confessed that spending time with Damian had made him feel broody. 'I can increasingly see the attraction of being a father,' he said. 'I like the idea of focusing on someone else.' But despite their closeness, friends cannot see them ever becoming a couple again because at the end of the day, Liz no longer fancies Hugh.

'I know I'll never stop loving Hugh, and if we're meant to get back together, we will,' she said in December 2000. But fundamentally their relationship remains rooted in friendship and their shared careers. 'He still reads my scripts if I've got offers and he always sends me his scripts to read,' she says. 'Before I go on the *David Letterman Show* I'll run my jokes past him. Before he does Leno, he'll tell me what he's going to say and I'll say, "Yeah, but it would be funnier if you say this." We've always helped each other.' Hugh Grant has never enjoyed the intense media scrutiny that comes with fame and is in no hurry to become Mr Liz Hurley again. She may have claimed in an interview with the *Observer* that she 'can't think of anything nicer in the world than being extremely successful and remaining anonymous', but the day she stops enjoying being photographed will be the day she stops being Liz Hurley. One has only to look at the photographs of the two of them in St Moritz to see their different reactions to the camera. There was Hugh Grant, head resolutely down, slight scowl on his face as he walked past the photographers who haunt the resort. And then there was Liz, immaculately made up, wearing sunglasses and a fur hat and looking radiant as she went on a sleigh ride through the winter wonderland.

And while she may moan that being a mother makes it difficult to meet new partners, in reality there is no shortage of men queuing up to date her. She is an attractive woman and an accomplished flirt. An American musician recalls being thrown up against the wall and French-kissed by Liz during a Sunday lunch party at his home in Los Angeles in the early 1990s. His wife was in the house at the time but that made no difference to Elizabeth the sexual predator. Since giving birth to Damian she has been linked to – among others – old Etonian Charles Dean, a millionaire racing driver who lives around the corner from her in Chelsea, and German socialite Sven Ley. In February 2003, her latest boyfriend was Arun Nayar, a wealthy, married playboy. He was with her in St Moritz and Liz chose to première him before the world's photographers at the Christian Dior fashion show in Paris. Sitting almost on top of her handsome date, Liz held hands and whispered into his ear throughout the show. They have also been seen lunching on each other's tongues in a London restaurant.

But friends expressed their concern that she may be heading for heartache again by falling in love with another spoilt rich boy. The 37-year-old, who is half Indian, half German, has a wife, and – like Steve Bing – a reputation as a womanizer. Heir to a textiles fortune, he enjoys an expensive jet-set lifestyle, with a penthouse apartment in Bombay's most exclusive area. He is currently living apart from his Italian-born model wife Valentina, but significantly did not see fit to tell her about his romance with Elizabeth. People who know him describe him as an enthusiastic member of the international jet set whose high-handed manner has upset more than a few people. 'I know him and he is an obnoxious and arrogant brat,' says Bombay news-paper columnist Shoba De, commenting in the *Daily Mail*. 'He is trading on his good looks.' Party guests were surprised to see him order Liz to fetch him a drink at a recent soirée in London, and watched incredulously as she obediently trotted off to do as she was told. But people who have known her for a long time know that she has always liked to be kept on her toes by a man. She finds being dominated a turn-on. When she was going out with Thomas Arklie, she enjoyed the fact that he wore the trousers in their relationship and kept her guessing about his feelings for her. Her constant fear that he might dump her only added to his appeal for her. It was the same with Steve Bing, whom she beguiled but ultimately failed to tame. In fact, the only man she has not had that type of relationship with was Hugh Grant. She bossed Grant around for years, with the result that she ceased to find him a turn-on sexually.

Liz has earned enough from modelling, advertising and film work to buy herself a £2 million house in Chelsea and a country retreat. But she has roamed from man to man and one can't help but wonder if she will ever marry. 'I think a man would be mad to marry a successful actress,' she once said. 'And I would not like to be a mousy little wife married to a famous film star.' Only a wealthy man would be able to keep up with her jet-set lifestyle and preferably wouldn't be bothered by boring things such as having to go to work. 'It's quite hard to date a civilian, because actresses are never in the same country for long and it would be quite hard to see someone who is a vet, for example, with a practice in Wiltshire,' she explained. 'They can't come to South Africa for three months, or California for six months. It's kind of difficult. You really wouldn't see them.'

Once described as 'an actress so wooden that when she films an outside scene they have to coat her in Ronseal', she also stands at a crossroads in her career. Her film biography reads like a who's who of movie turkeys – *Beyond Bedlam*, *Mad Dogs and Englishmen* and *Dawg* to name but a few – and it has been said that the only way she will ever get her hands on an Oscar is if she is asked to polish one. With her latest two movies being panned in America and going straight to video in the UK, her acting career is in crisis. '*Weight of Water* sank without trace,' says Sean Macaulay. 'Her acting is not going to go anywhere. She is regarded as being decorative, basically.' As the 1998 Channel 5 documentary *This Wonderful World* concluded about her, Liz is made for phootgraphic stills. She just doesn't seem to be much good in moving pictures.

In early 2003, she and her friend Denis Leary came close to tying up a deal to produce their own TV show in America. It could have propelled Liz into the big league of TV high-earners and in time may even have put her on a par with *Frasier* star Jane Leeves. But the deal fell through when she allegedly demanded too much money. Executives at NBC television were interested in the concept of *Nerve*, a legal drama which Liz would also star in, and asked her to sign for six episodes. But when she apparently asked for £140,000 for each one they axed the entire project. It was a crushing blow for someone whose last few movies have failed to set the screen alight. Celebrity watcher Marc Freden says Hurley may have over-estimated her standing in Hollywood. 'In all honesty, I don't think there's a huge perception of her, period,' he says. 'People in England forget just how big the industry is here and just how hard a nut it is to crack. There is a pecking order to stardom. At the top are the legendary stars, people like Elizabeth Taylor and Kirk Douglas, who are the real Hollywood royalty. Then there are the power stars, like Tom Cruise and Julia Roberts and Tom Hanks – A-list stars who are at the top of the heap. Then it goes down to the lesser stars, B-list actors like Kevin Spacey and James Woods who are on the same level as the really big television stars like Jerry Seinfeld or the casts of *Friends* and *ER*. Then there are lesser television stars and C-list movie stars, and then character actors.

'Elizabeth Hurley falls into the category of being famous for being famous and is certainly less important than A- and B-list TV stars. If you asked the average person on the street if they recognized her they'd say "Oh, yeah", but if you said her name they might not get it. That's the curse of being a model, your face is everywhere. What do you think if you think Elizabeth Hurley? You think: model, you think Versace, and you think Hugh Grant. It's not that she's not well thought of; she's just not thought of at all in this town. Do you really think you're going to see Elizabeth Hurley any time soon playing somebody's mother? She doesn't have that kind of diversity. If she truly wants to be an actress she should go and learn how to act.'

It is the production company that she runs with Hugh Grant that probably offers Elizabeth the best chance of long-term security. 'Simian Films should be diversifying and I think she's smart enough to know that,' says Freden. 'If the company isn't just worried about making star vehicles for Elizabeth Hurley, she could work as an executive – a power-wielder – for perpetuity. But I don't think she's considered even as a filmmaker. The fact is, women have a harder slog in this town.'

Elizabeth's prospects as a model look only slightly rosier. For the time being, her future with Estée Lauder remains secure and she signed a new three-year contract with the company early in 2003. She may also front an advertising campaign for Versace, with which she retains a close association. But modelling is a young person's game and with a few notable exceptions not many women continue to be offered work once they hit forty. It is no coincidence that Liz's Estée Lauder contract is due to expire six months after she turns 40 in June 2006. The effort involved in looking as good as she does is phenomenal and often grim. 'You have to be disciplined,' she says. 'You have to want a small bottom more than you want a cake. If you want the cake more than the bottom, then forget about it – you're not going to be thin.' It is the sort of frank honesty that makes women particularly appreciate just how much effort goes into keeping her looking as good as she does. When she lived with Hugh Grant, he always insisted that she eat a proper meal. Once they parted she would skip dinner and make do with pretzels and wine. But will she still want to subject herself to cold (toning) showers and fat-free watercress soup when she is in middle age? The answer is yes because to keep her star image, she needs to appear glamorous.

That also costs a hell of a lot of money. 'If Elizabeth stops flying first class, she's over, and she knows it,' says a fashion editor. This is one of the reasons why the gold-digger accusations appeared to stick so easily. To many, the received wisdom is thus: a model in her late 30s, facing a declining career, looks for security in the arms of a rich man – Bingo! It certainly seems unlikely that Liz will ever settle for a poor man. 'I would definitely say that she is on the make,' says former lover Will Annesley. 'I mean, look at the boyfriends since Hugh Grant: Teddy Forstmann, Steve Bing – they have all been serious players. These people don't fly first class; you're talking private jet. That kind of power and that kind of money puts you into a different echelon. Movie stars are small potatoes compared to these guys.'

Those who have known her over the years speak of a bossy, driven, woman who can be enormous fun to be around. Her sister, who perhaps knows her best of all, describes her as secretive and never content. 'One of my nicknames for her is Divine Discontent, which is a character from one of Evelyn Waugh's books,' she once said. 'She's incredibly well meaning. To the people she cares for, she's the most loyal, most loving person you will ever meet, spectacularly kind and generous. Her heart is definitely in the right place. But if someone annoys Elizabeth she just won't bother to speak to them.' This removal of affection is something that Hugh Grant also uses to cutting effect. 'If he withdraws his charm, which he does like he's knocked a switch, you feel yourself in a very cold place indeed,' one of his friends from Oxford told his biographer Jody Tresidder. 'But when the sun peeps out again in Hugh, it shines on everyone.'

Like the majority of famous people, Liz has made her fair share of enemies over the years. Her former friend Charlotte Lewis describes her as a nasty piece of work and her conduct during the SAG dispute has led to a certain amount of lingering hostility towards her in Hollywood. 'People think she's a bit calculating,' admits Birgit Cunningham. 'They see her at premières in lovely dresses and forget that underneath she is a really great person who anyone would just love to hang out with. She's great fun. She's got a very good sense of humour and she's very thoughtful about people. Because she is very confident in her sexuality it is easy to criticize her and dismiss her as a slapper. But I actually think it's a bit unfair. I think it would be a bit boring if we all wore grey cardigans the whole time. If anyone says anything bad about her it's usually because their boyfriends want her and they're jealous. I think she is someone that people should really admire and look up to. She's got all the great things about a career-woman but she's also gorgeous and sexy. She has become such an icon that, looking back, it was like living with Elvis.'

But her first boyfriend doesn't share Cunningham's flattering opinion. Antony Allcock, he who was formerly known as Septic, has watched Liz's meteoric rise to fame with a cynical eye. 'Sad to say that her head has now gone up her backside,' he says bluntly. 'I feel very sad for her because it feels like she's sold herself out and burnt herself out. And she didn't need to do that. She's gone for the Hollywood stuff. She's got a lot of bucks and if that's what she was after, then fine. But if it's not, then it's a sad day, isn't it?'

She continues to make headlines on an almost daily basis, whether she is appearing half-naked on the front cover of *Vogue* with her legs wrapped around Elton John's neck, or holding hands with her latest squeeze. *The Scotsman* described her as a 'flashbulb courtesan who enslaves the paparazzi like no British woman since Princess Diana', and while it is true that there are many actresses who are more talented than her, and also more beautiful, Liz Hurley's image has struck gold. She is a dichotomy – a woman who poses topless for the men's magazine *Esquire* and in the same article brands men who leer at lap-dancers 'oiks and half-wits'. She may not be a 'girl's girl' but it is this ballsy attitude which makes women admire Elizabeth Hurley.

She remains remarkably self-effacing where her looks are concerned. 'Some days I think I wash up well, but then I look pale and tired,' she says. 'I think beauty is more about emotional quality. You know – kind eyes, that sort of thing.' She cheerfully admits that magazine photographs of her are routinely retouched, saying, 'No woman has thighs like that!' Asked in 1999 if she feared losing the looks that made her, she replied, 'No, not really.' And on the subject of face-lifts she said, 'I don't find it attractive and it doesn't really make you look any younger. You can't take that path unless you want a life of despondency.' She insists that she has done what every woman can do and simply made the best of what God gave her. 'I've learned every trick in the book when it comes to eliminating the negatives,' she said. 'You don't have to be Einstein to work out what to accentuate and what to disguise at all costs. When I had my eyebrows shaped, people thought that I'd had a face-lift. That's what a difference eyebrows make.' But looking at photographs of her over the years, at least one surgeon concluded that she has used collagen to make her lips fuller, and has also used botox.

But whatever it is that she does, millions of women are desperate to know her secret. Personal trainers are inundated with women who want to look like her, and cosmetic surgeons are continually asked by their clients, 'Give me lips like Liz Hurley.' But her zealous commitment to the body beautiful has come at a price. The famous Hurley boobs, most beloved of the tabloid press and arguably her greatest asset, appear to have all but disappeared. 'Missing: Liz's boobs,' wailed *The Sun* newspaper. 'Have you seen these?' it asked its readers, under a photograph of Liz's pre-diet cleavage. One thing is certain: if and when they reappear their return will be warmly welcomed.

Chapter 10

And at the end of the day, it doesn't really matter if Elizabeth Hurley is not a good actress because Liz Hurley, her more successful alter ego, is a star through and through.